A
SACRED HIGH
PLACE

I0211493

A
SACRED HIGH PLACE

A HISTORY OF
MOUNT CARMEL
CEMETERY
& MEETINGHOUSE
McNAIRY COUNTY, TENNESSEE

Including an Updated Census
of the Cemetery

John E. Talbott, J.D.

BRAYBREE
Publishing

Copyright © 2013 John E. Talbott, J.D.
All rights reserved

Published by BrayBree Publishing Company LLC
FIRST EDITION

No part of this book may be reproduced, stored in or introduced into a retrieval system or transmitted in any form or by any means (electronic, mechanical, photocopying, recording, or otherwise) without the prior written permission of the copyright owner.

The scanning, uploading, and distribution of this book on the Internet or through any other means is not permitted without permission from the copyright owner.

Front cover and frontispiece: John Robert McIntyre and Sarah (McIntyre) Fowler, with Ollie Pearl (McCann) McIntyre and J.R. McIntyre to the right.

ISBN: 978-0-9671251-9-0

Printed in the United States of America

BrayBree Publishing Company LLC
P.O. Box 1204
Dickson, Tennessee 37056-1204
Visit our website at www.braybreepublishing.com

Dedication

*To the pioneering citizens of north McNairy County
who lie in eternal slumber in Mount Carmel Cemetery,
and to their pioneering spirit which allowed them
to build a community out of a wilderness
in hopes that their descendants shall honor that spirit
by preserving their history.*

CONTENTS

ACKNOWLEDGEMENTS

Anytime an individual pens a book, he owes many an acknowledgment. In a book like this, which was compiled and accumulated over a period of twenty years or more, it is difficult to acknowledge everyone who has assisted in some manner or another over the years. So many individuals contributed some small but vital bit of information that not all could be identified. I wish here to collectively thank all of those, both living and dead, who shared with me some vital clue to the lives represented in historic old Mount Carmel Cemetery. However, I would like to thank a few individual people specifically.

First, I wish to acknowledge my father, Ronald L. Talbott, who long ago taught me the importance of maintaining and improving the resting places of the dead. His example in seeking to improve Mount Carmel and other such burying grounds has made it easier for succeeding generations to care for those grounds. Second, I wish

x ACKNOWLEDGEMENTS

to thank Mr. Richard Leath, the gentleman who tirelessly worked to build the seed money of the current trust. His continued efforts over many years paved the way for future progress. Third, I would like to acknowledge the talents and hard work of my co-publisher, Kevin McCann, who also shares a special interest in Mount Carmel Cemetery. It was Kevin's talent and hard work in designing and setting up the book that gave it the look it carries.

Finally, I wish to thank my wife Michelle and my two daughters, Ava Jewel and Claire Elisabeth. These three wonderful ladies gave me the time and opportunity to work on this book despite many wishes to the contrary. They sacrifice much in the way of time so I can pursue the study and preservation of local history for the benefit of future generations like their own. To Michelle, Ava, and Claire, I am ever grateful!

JOHN E. TALBOTT, J.D.

PREFACE

The history of the Mount Carmel Cemetery and Meetinghouse is not particularly shrouded in mystery. Indeed, there are some aspects to its history that remain an enigma to us even today in the twenty-first century. However, its history and tradition are as known to us as any other cemetery's history or tradition can be. Like many cemeteries, it has had more than one meetinghouse over the years and those meetinghouses have been affiliated with at least two different religious denominations. The cemetery has more than its fair share of unmarked and unknown graves. However, unlike others of its era, many graves in recent years have been reclaimed and marked. It has also benefited from private interest and a desire by a few to preserve its historical integrity.

Its history is rich because of many of the characters buried in it. These people may not have been financially wealthy, but they were among the leaders of their times. Buried at Mount Carmel are public office holders and politicians, soldiers of various wars (especially the American Civil War), farmers, merchants, entrepreneurs, educators, a physician, a hobo, and scores of others of varying occupations. The celebration at Mount Carmel has ranged from a large colorful event to honor the dead to modern-day reunions that may vary from successful to sparsely attended, depending upon the year.

Young attendees have grown into elderly attendees and enjoyed the Decoration Day one year, only to be among the honored dead interred there on the old hill by the time of the next Decoration. Old families whose members visited for generations have passed into eternity and have no one left to celebrate their lives. New families have established roots nearby. The march of time has continued uninterrupted. New graves appear periodically. The grass grows and the tombstones weather and crumble.

Still, efforts are being made to preserve the past at Mount Carmel so that younger generations may learn and appreciate the sacrifices of those hardy settlers buried on this hallowed ground. There is an old adage that nothing stays the same. That is true. The cemetery and the current meeting house will either deteriorate or they will be revitalized and persevered. However, revitalization and preservation doesn't happen without hard work, funds, and a vision for the future. The Mount Carmel Perpetual Preservation and Care Foundation, Inc. was recently established to ensure that the cemetery and meetinghouse would be protected in years to come and free from the danger of outside influences and squatters, a fate that has befallen some of its sister churches and cemeteries in recent years.

Creation of the corporation and its stewardship of the cemetery and meetinghouse will prevent the occupation of the property by some outside individual who takes advantage of the perception that a cemetery or meetinghouse has been abandoned. The public can rest assured that Mount Carmel has not been abandoned. It continues to be maintained, preserved, and carefully attended to after more than 185 years. Historical and structural preservation and documentation are now going to be the concentration of the efforts at Mount Carmel. Mowing grass and landscaping will be just a necessary secondary chore. It does little good to mow around crumbling and illegible mounds of ancient limestone and marble. The identities and integrity of the individual graves must be maintained and enhanced in order for future generations to understand the importance of this special spot of earth.

The current meetinghouse is being preserved in order to serve an educational role and to provide a place for gathering during the annual Decoration Day. Eventually, the meetinghouse will house a photographic and historical display to give visitors to Decoration Day an understanding of the history of the community, the cemetery itself, and the people interred therein. The goal of these projects is to leave behind the legacy of a proud heritage in which one's forbearers are honored and remembered. It is the author's hope that all will seek to share in this endeavor.

JOHN E. TALBOTT, J.D.

CHAPTER ONE

HISTORY OF THE
MOUNT CARMEL CEMETERY

According to tradition and some written historical sources, Mount
Carmel was originally settled by Matthew and Esther Ward when
the couple pitched a tent on the old hill and set out an orchard. As with all
new settlers in a new area, the Wards picked a high place above a source
of water. Near them were Billie's Creek, Hogwallow Creek, and Huggins
Creek. In 1823, Huggins Creek was already recognized as Hugganses
Creek, probably having been named by a member of the surveying party
exploring the region after it was acquired from the Chickasaw Nation.[1]
The Wards had migrated from North Carolina and were looking to make
a new life in the territories gained following the Jackson Purchase Trea-
ty of 1818. According to sources in 1927, Matthew Ward established a
habitation there on Mount Carmel.[2] It was likely a log structure and that

1. McNairy County, Tennessee Register of Deeds Office, Deed Book A, page 2.
2. *McNairy County Independent Appeal*, May 20, 1927.

structure may very well have been the first meetinghouse located on the spot. Of course this is speculation, but it remains a possibility. There are no historical sources to give us more particular and accurate information as to the establishment of the first meetinghouse.

We do not know the circumstances of Matthew and Esther Ward's further movements in McNairy County, but apparently they did abandon Mount Carmel hill for another more suitable homestead at some point thereafter. Mount Carmel Cemetery was first laid out in or about 1825 or 1826, according to early historical sources.[3] Most sources attribute the first burial as that of Abram Lorance (Lowrance).[4] Oral tradition has it that the first man to be buried in Mount Carmel was cutting wheat not far from that hill and became very hot. Accordingly, the man drank too much water and then suffered something like a heat stroke from his exposure and overexertion.[5] The second grave was said to be that of a Mrs. Tabbie White.[6] There was a Tabitha Hodges White in the vicinity of Mount Carmel. She was the daughter of Elisha and Amilla (Millie) Ward Hodges and married Samuel White, who is perhaps buried in Mount Carmel Cemetery himself, though this cannot currently be verified. However, if Tabitha Hodges White is Mrs. Tabbie White, there is an issue that cannot be readily resolved. Tabitha did not die until the 1850s and there are old markers in the cemetery with death dates indi-

---

3. *Id.*

4. A September 8, 1922, article in the *McNairy County Independent Appeal* concerning Mt. Carmel identified Abram Lowrance as being the first grave there "about 100 years ago." Interestingly enough, General Wright mentioned an Abram Lorance, stating that he came to McNairy county in 1824 and lived to an old age, of about 90 to 100 years. There is nothing to suggest that they are the same Abram Lorance. There is the possibility that two Abrams existed, one the father and the other the son. However, such speculation will serve only as a possibility which the reader is free to consider and subsequently accept or reject.

5. This story was passed to the author from various sources including members of the McIntyre family. However if this is the same Abram Lorance as mentioned by General Wright, it is doubtful that Lorance, at such an advanced age, would be cutting wheat.

6. *Id.* This article mentioned that this Tabbie White was the great-grandmother of Mrs. John Tedford.

cating death in the 1830s. Therefore, if the two were one and the same, then she was not the second occupant of Mount Carmel Cemetery.[7]

Regardless of the identity of the first or second individuals to be buried in the cemetery, it should be noted that Mount Carmel is one of the oldest burying grounds in the county. The oldest marked grave today is that of Susana Lowrance, the wife of Jacob Lowrance (October 14, 1814–April 19, 1837). Interestingly, her grave and that of her husband, who died some 45 years afterwards, are located quite some space apart. In the center area of the current cemetery, there exists a large void. One should not be fooled about this area. In fact, probing and other methods show that the area is completely occupied with old graves. Sunken graves often appear in this portion of the cemetery and portions of old cedar stumps still lie just under the soil.[8] As the cemetery, like all cemeteries, started small and grew beyond its original boundaries, there may have been no room for the Lowrances to be buried next to one another. Similarly, the Hodges family is buried in two separate portions of the cemetery. Those infants and small children lost in early childhood by the Putmans, Elijah J. Hodges, and Captain Horry Hodges are buried far away in the cemetery from their parents.

Three different articles have been written concerning the old cemetery, one in 1922, another in 1927, and a final article in 1934. Each of these will be reprinted here with any appropriate notes. The following article appeared in the *McNairy County Independent Appeal* on September 8, 1922. It was probably authored by Will K. Abernathy or Orpheus Abernathy upon a visit to the cemetery during the graveside services for the late Professor Harvey G. Hodges.[9]

---

7. At the time that the article was written, many older graves were still marked by cedar trees and sandstone rocks and several tombstones that would later be damaged or destroyed by the logging of the cemetery's cedar trees were still intact. It may have been that Mrs. Tabbie White's marker was the next oldest marker in the cemetery. Still, even then there is a problem in that Susana Lowrance's marker, which existed in 1927, reflects an 1837 death date.

8. The reader may recall that in poorer and simpler times, families did not have either the funds or access to carved limestone or marble monuments. Instead, they planted cedar trees at the head and foot of new graves. Cedars grew slowly but into large trees that could act as a semi-permanent monuments. Some families erected flat sandstones as headstones or footstones.

9. A more detailed sketch of Professor Hodges appears in Chapter Three.

We visited this historic burying ground on the occasion of the funeral of Harvey Hodges, and within its confines rest the ashes of many of the county's oldest and most respected citizens. It is situated on an eminence overlooking the valleys surrounding it, east of the railroad, and southeast of the town of Finger. The first grave made there was that of Abram Lowrance about 100 years ago and the second was that of Mrs. Tabbie White, the great-grandmother of Mrs. John Tedford. On the weather-stained side of an old monument chiseled by the sculptor many years ago we found the inscription "Mrs. Rebecca Bullner, born in 1789, and died in 1855." The grandfather of W.J. Clayton, Jessie Clayton, sleeps in the old cemetery, as do the father and mother of Esq. J.S. Lain, Thomas Lain, born in 1807, dying in 1886, and Jane Lain, born in 1821, dying in 1879. We found the monument of Dave Owen, showing him to have been born in 1810, dying in 1885. There in the silent tomb sleep the remains of the grandfather of Wash Gage, Bobby McIntyre, and scores of others of the older citizens who aided in the upbuilding of the county.[10] What a wonderful history is held in these silent and ever sacred places and what recollections of other days come upon all of us when we read these lettered monuments.

Mount Carmel in the olden times had associated with it the name of Elijah, the prophet. In this Mount Carmel there is the association of another Elijah, Elijah Hodges, father of the deceased, who in his day was a tower of strength in the Primitive Baptist Church, with which church Harvey Hodges had been identified for many years.

The following article, entitled "Mt. Carmel Memorial" is taken from the May 20, 1927 edition of the *McNairy County Independent Appeal*. Once again it is very likely the author of this article is one or another of the Abernathy family, the publishers and editors of the newspaper. However, it is possible that a close friend of that family, the Honorable

10. Bobby McIntyre most likely refers to Robert Thompson McIntyre (1814–1902), who was the great-great-great grandfather of the author, and is buried at Mount Carmel.

Horry Hodges, could have written it. However, because it is unsigned, it is more probable that one of the editors is the true author.

> A large crowd assembled at old Mt. Carmel last Sunday for an all-day memorial service. It was an ideal day. Parker preached an interesting sermon in the morning. A most sumptuous dinner, just such as the good women in that community are in the habit of spreading, was served. In the afternoon the many graves in the old cemetery were decorated. There was a song service. W.K. and Terry Abernathy delivered brief memorial addresses and Horry Hodges was master of ceremonies.
>
> Mt. Carmel is one of the oldest burying grounds in the county. It was laid out as such in 1825. It is on an eminence, with gentle slopes all around. Nature has provided perfect drainage. Nearby is the old church building in which so many of the funeral services have been held, and where the old time ministers of the Gospel preached in the years that are gone in their good, old-fashioned way.[11]
>
> In this cemetery sleep the ashes of the early pioneers and settlers of that section. Matthew Ward, great grandfather of J.G. Ward, pitched his tent and established a habitation on these grounds in the early twenties of the last century. There he set out his orchards, and built his humble home in the then wilderness. Others joined him and a settlement was formed. Death visited the settlement and into the bosom of old Mt. Carmel were laid the remains of this first one to answer the summons; the old cemetery is almost filled with the graves of the old and the young.
>
> The writer strolled through it; he read from the lettered monuments a history of the past one hundred years and more of McNairy county; one of toil and labor and sacrifice.

---

11. The old church building to which reference is made is the building immediately preceding the current cinder block building. This structure was in extreme disrepair by the 1930s. The building, by that time, was void of windows and doors and was leaning precariously. This building was dismantled in the early 1940s and the current structure was erected.

There was a plain slab and on it was the chiseled name of
Rebecca Bullner, and the record, born in 1789, died in 1855.[12]
And another monument to David Bullner born in 1814, died
in 1898. There was one in memory of an old preacher, Rev.
W.A. McHalstead, born in 1808, died in 1891; that of his
companion Elizabeth, born in 1809, died in 1886. There was
a monument at the grave of Jacob Lorance, a pioneer and former trustee of the county, born in 1803, died in 1882. And
there was the monument in memory of Hugh and Lige Kirkpatrick, brothers who walked the uncharted way from North
Carolina and settled in that section nearly a century ago. There
is one in memory of the Carrolls, the Harris brothers, Henry
and Pink; to the Owens, and Covey.

In the north end of the cemetery are the graves of Capt.
E.J. Hodges, and his faithful companion. Monuments mark
their resting places. He was born in 1831 and died in 1913,
and his companion was born in 1834 and died in 1921. Capt.
Hodges was another of the old-time preachers; a stalwart
citizen. Then we saw the monument at the grave of their son,
Harvey G. Hodges. He was born in 1876 and died in 1922.
We saw the monument at the grave of Jim Wright Hodges.
He was born in 1857 and died in 1916. There was a monument at the grave of W.W. Peeples. He was once a member
of the county court, born in 1850 and died in 1902.

There is double monument in memory of J.F. Putman, who
was born in 1841 and died in 1921, and his wife, who was born
in 1844 and died in 1922. The monument at the grave of Robert M. Clayton shows he was born in 1827 and died in 1863.

12. Strangely enough, both articles mention Rebecca Bulliner and both articles misspell her
name.

We saw the grave of Francis M. Clayton, an old citizen and at one time justice of the peace.[13] In another part of the cemetery we saw three old graves flower-strewn and unmarked. They were of the Lowreys of the family of Gen. Mark Lowrey, who resided near this place in the early part of the last century. The Lowreys of Mississippi are of this family.

It is a beautiful custom to assemble on these annual memorial occasions, and take part in all the services. To scatter upon the graves of loved ones the sweet flowers of the springtime is a fitting and tender tribute, an expression of the love and affection we have for loved ones sleeping in these cities of the dead."

The article writer indicates that Mount Carmel was the beginning of a settlement and that the cemetery was the first burying ground into which these settlers were interred. Given the area's geography, it makes sense that a settlement could thrive there. Mount Carmel is located on a high prominence (for West Tennessee landscapes) rising above fertile and flat farm land and two creeks fed by natural springs. It may well have been that early pioneer life in what is now the Finger, Tennessee area centered on and around Mount Carmel. After all, we know that Hugh Kerby was born near the spot of his burial at Mount Carmel. Further, we know that he was the first white child born in McNairy County, Tennessee. There were very few burying grounds in the first four or five decades of the area's settlement. The ones known to exist from 1823 to 1850 include Mount Carmel, White Plains, Floyd, Hendrix, and Plunk Cemeteries. Although some of these cemeteries have strong family contingencies buried within them, hence their names, they also served as community cemeteries and all are separated by several miles. There are other small family cemeteries predating 1850, but they are quite small

13. Interestingly, both monuments currently marking the grave of Francis Marion Clayton were erected sometime long after 1927. In fact, his Confederate service monument was not erected until sometime around or shortly after the year 2000. However, at the time of this article's writing, the cemetery was full of large, majestic, and old cedar trees. According to sources contemporary at the time of the cutting of those trees including L.E. and Faye Talbott, Lessie McIntyre, Roy McIntyre, Vivian McIntyre, Guy Brown, and others, several older monuments were destroyed when the old trees were felled. Thereafter, the broken monuments were carried off and buried nearby. Indeed, these articles mention graves no longer marked and discernible.

and confined to one family. These pre-1850 cemeteries include those for the Anderson, Ingraham, and Kerby families.

Finally, the last column regarding Mount Carmel Cemetery was typed on a piece of stationery belonging to the St. Louis Police Veterans' Association, St. Louis, Missouri. It is dated August 9, 1958, and is entitled "Reprint of Memorial Day at Mt. Carmel, Sunday, May 20, 1934." The following statement is found at the top of the document: "I, William S. McIntyre, was at the Decoration day, Sunday, May 18, 1958, and the same usual crowd was there but only a few missing each time; a very large crowd was present." This is Sam McIntyre, son of James Robert McIntyre and grandson of Robert Thompson McIntyre. The article reprint states as follows:

> Sunday, May 20, 1934, a great crowd assembled at Mt. Carmel in the 8th District to observe the annual memorial and Decoration Day in the old burying ground. The day was ideal and the people there assembled took a keen interest in the proceedings. Horry Hodges, whose ancestors sleep in this burying ground, was master of ceremonies, and in his usual happy manner, carried out the program. His address, historical and reminiscent, was enjoyed by all. W.K. Abernathy, who had been invited to deliver a memorial address, was present and spoke briefly.
>
> Mt. Carmel was laid out as a country graveyard in 1826, one hundred and eight years ago. It was so named by the old pioneers, who were students of the Bible and who were familiar with these old Testament characters.
>
> In that cemetery sleep the remains of Elijah Hodges, a celebrated Primitive Baptist Minister in the early days of the county. He received his name from parents who knew the history of Biblical Mt. Carmel and of the part that Elijah of old played on the summit of the mountain far removed from old Jerusalem. His devoted companion sleeps beside him there in the sanctuary of the tomb in Mt. Carmel, and others of the blood sleep there also. Not only do these good old people rest there, but it is the final resting place of others of these pioneers. We recall the names of the Youngs, Harris, Womble,

Kirkpatrick, Barham, Naylor, Lowery, Lain, Malone, Carroll, and Cook.

When this burying ground was laid out, McNairy county had just been established a year before, in 1825.[14] Within the confines of the Mt. Carmel burying grounds are many imposing monuments. There are rough grave stones that mark the graves of many of the old settlers who found honored sepulture in old Mt. Carmel.

On the polished surface of some of these monuments are chiseled the names of those whose graves are marked by these monuments, erected by loving hands in memory of some departed loved ones. While these rough crude stones bear no inscriptions, they are none the less tokens of the love and affection of those who placed them there. We saw great cedar trees that had been set out by some loving hand a long time ago. They shade the ground and in season and out, bear mute, but eloquent testimony to the undying love of a father, mother, husband, wife or child, for someone whose remains sleep in the soil at Mt. Carmel. We have been to Mt. Carmel before on memorial occasions. But the occasion last Sunday was one of the most impressive of any.

Flowers were placed upon all the graves, and besides, there were flowers then blooming in the wildest profusion where some loving hand had planted them in the years that are gone.

It is interesting to note that the first white child born in McNairy county was Hugh Kerby. The child grew to manhood, and his remains now repose in Mt. Carmel. This old settler is the grandfather of Mrs. Mary Lain Malone, whose father was the late J.S. Lain. Another interesting bit of history is that in the graveyard are the remains of the ancestors of Gen. M.P. Lowery who served with Gen. Forrest in the Civil War. Gen. Lowery was a Brigadier General at 33 and a Major General at 35.[15]

14. This is incorrect, as the county was formed in 1823.

15. Again there is some inaccuracy in this account. General Mark Perrin Lowery rose to the rank of brigadier general at the age of 35, the highest rank he attained in the Confederate Army.

Mount Carmel Cemetery. The tombstone in the foreground is that of Nancy James, and the one in the background is Nancy Caroline McIntyre. Note the large cedar trees inside the cemetery.

This concludes the text of the surviving three articles which have been written concerning the old Mount Carmel Cemetery. However, there is a great deal more to discuss concerning this old hallowed ground.

From 1826 to 1900, the cemetery continued to grow as the settlement of this section of the county progressed. Families continued their westward migration from states such as North Carolina, South Carolina and Virginia. The old, the weak, the sick and the newborn died as the rigors of the pioneer life took their toll. With these sad and tragic events, the cemetery grew. As one can imagine, the cemetery remained on private property. Of course, the owner did not object to burials and allowed the plot of land to be used. The land on which it was located then swapped hands, i.e. title was transferred over the years, and in time additional land was needed for the growing cemetery.

Between 1826 and 1870, the cemetery grew and the land remained in private hands. However, by 1870, with a thriving congregation meeting at the meetinghouse, now known as the Mount Carmel Methodist

Protestant Church, and a cemetery yard growing each year, the need arose to place the property into the hands of trustees. The owner of the ground at the time was Harmon Purdy Floyd and he conveyed the cemetery and meetinghouse grounds to the trustees of the Mount Carmel Methodist Protestant Church. Those trustees were Robert Z. Henderson, P.A. Brown, William M. Crow and William H. Stinson.[16] At the time, the minister at the Mount Carmel Church was the Reverend Wilson A. McHolstead.

The property conveyed to the trustees was as follows:

> BEING a part of Entry No. 2221 for two acres including the Mount Carmel Church and Graveyard beginning at the Northwest corner in said tract on a black oak white oak and Spanish oak pointers running East 18 poles to a black oak and Spanish oak and chestnut pointers then South 18 poles to a stake black jack and red oak and hickory pointers then West 18 poles to a stake 2 black jack pointers thence North to the Beginning containing by estimation two acres be the same more or less.

The deed was attested to by the Reverend McHolstead and was executed on August 16, 1870. The deed may be found of record in Deed Book K, Page 758 in the Register's Office of McNairy County, Tennessee.

Between 1870 and 1904, the cemetery continued to grow as the community grew. By the turn of the twentieth century, the village of Finger was beginning to take shape and experienced a boom cycle within a decade. Further, there appeared to be a need for building a new meetinghouse. By this time, the ground occupied by graves and needed for expansion was owned by local farmer and widow Mary Roberta McIntyre. The property conveyed by Mrs. McIntyre was as follows:

> BEGINNING at the S.E. corner of said graveyard (Mt. Carmel Graveyard) and runs south 9 poles to a stake; thence West 18 poles to a stake; thence north 9 poles to a stake or N.W. corner of said graveyard (Mt. Carmel Graveyard); thence East 18 poles to the beginning, containing one acre. The purpose

16. P.A. Brown was Pleasant A. Brown, the paternal great-grandfather of Mr. Guy Brown.

of this gift is for the purpose of enlarging said yard and for building a church house on same.

This conveyance was made by warranty deed and was executed by Mrs. McIntyre on August 26, 1904, and was given to certain unnamed patrons. Interestingly, this deed was held by some party and was not recorded until almost forty-four years later on July 23, 1948. It was recorded in Deed Book 42, page 86 in the Register's Office of McNairy County, Tennessee.

The final conveyance to the cemetery came about as a result of changes to the course of Mount Carmel Road in the 1930s. Once the road took on its present course, there was an issue of access from the new road to the cemetery itself. J.E. "Ed" Stephens and wife Amanda "Mandy" Stephens owned land adjoining the cemetery, and their land proved to be a barrier between the new road and the cemetery. The Stephens conveyed the following property to the trustees of the Mount Carmel graveyard:

> BEGINNING at iron stake the northwest corner of J.E. Stephens tract of land and on the South line of P.E. Wharton, runs east 116 poles to a stake and black oak pointer, then South 30 feet to a stake, then west 116 poles to a stake, thence north 30 feet to the beginning, containing by estimation one acre and 52 Square rods, the purpose of this conveyance as a road right-of-way leading to Mount Carmel Grave Yard.

The property was conveyed to the cemetery trustees, who at that time included Harmon E. Hodges, W.L. Plunk, and Hugh Kirkpatrick. As stated above, the conveyance of this tract was for the purpose of creating a road right of way from the county road to the cemetery across that property owned in fee simple at that time by the Stephens. This conveyance was not for the purpose of constructing a private cemetery drive. This deed was executed on February 1, 1937, and of record in Deed Book 27, page 522 in the Register's Office of McNairy County, Tennessee.

Now back to those who found a home in the cemetery. Sometimes the very healthy and vigorous succumbed to accident and disease. Like many cemeteries of the era, in the confines of Mount Carmel Cemetery may be found numerous families that were struck by epidemic illnesses.

Members of the Hodges family on Decoration Day at Mount Carmel Cemetery

In some cases, mothers gave birth to children they would hold only in death, as mother and child would die in the process of childbirth. Between 1862 and 1865, many young men died of disease or wounds during the conflagration of the American Civil War. A few examples are in order to better demonstrate the fragility of life prior to the advent of medical technology after the turn of the twentieth century.

The reader will note that Nicy B. Clayton died giving birth to a daughter on February 21, 1873. Charles B. Covy died during his service to the Union Army during the American Civil War. Mary Roberta McIntyre and daughter Zenar McIntyre died during the 1907 typhoid fever outbreak. One other relative in the home with them died as well, but was buried elsewhere. George W. Bulliner was murdered on December 12, 1873, while residing in Illinois. His death sparked decades-long feuding in Williamson County, Illinois that caused it to become known as "Bloody Williamson." William Harrison Whitt died as a result of his own crime. He walked up behind a foe of his, grabbed him, and shot the man in the chest. The bullet traveled through the man and struck Whitt, killing him. Allen R. Womble was a young man working on the street cars in downtown Memphis when met his youthful death in a street car collision in 1909. These are just a few examples of the more spectacular ways that people leave the haunts of this earth.

A rather quick and brief review of the current census of the cemetery shows some startling rates of infant mortality and early childhood death. Prior to 1900, there were no less than 49 occurrences of infant mortality or early childhood death. There were no less than four deaths between the ages of 5 and 10 years. Finally, there were five deaths of adolescents between the ages of 10 and 18 years. By 1900 and afterwards, these numbers had declined in some instances. For example, infant mortality and early childhood death rates from 1900 until 1950 reflect 38 occurrences. Deaths of children between ages 5 and 10 years had fallen to two deaths. Deaths of young adolescents between ages of 10 and 18 years had risen to nine. Of course, these numbers are restricted to Mount Carmel Cemetery and only to its marked graves. However, these numbers are important. Collectively, they reflect that 107 persons or approximately 22% of the population buried in Mount Carmel died before the age of eighteen. Of that number, 87 died prior to the age of five and account for almost 18% of the graves in the cemetery.

The cemetery retained its original landscape and appearance until the late 1940s or early 1950s. During that period, someone made the decision to cut the large cedar trees in the cemetery. Most of the older locals maintained that Miss Maggie Hodges and Albert Owens made the decision to cut the old trees. Regardless, when they were cut, the felling of these trees resulted in the destruction of more than a few old tombstones. Few, if any, were apparently ever replaced.

Much well-intended but destructive activity took place during this period. There was a slave and black section on the west side of the present-day cemetery. Here in this separate section was the final resting place for slaves, former slaves, and other blacks. During a period as late as the late 1930s, it was enclosed by a white wooden fence and still being used. The exact location of these graves and the size of the black section is disputed. However, it appears to have been located at least partially where the cemetery drive was constructed. In other words, the black section was disturbed in order to build the drive. Although some of it may now be covered in woods, it likely begins in the bare and vacant looking area

Views of Mount Carmel Cemetery

around the edge of the west side of the cemetery.[17] Most who remember the black section recall it being well-kept and fairly large and may have included some tombstones. Regardless of its nature, it is a shame that such destruction has been done.

Over the years, the nature of grave keeping and maintenance has changed. During the earlier years of the twentieth century, many families enclosed their lots with brick and block in order to keep their lots themselves. For many years the cemetery was not uniformly maintained. People hauled white sand to the cemetery and mounded the graves to create a type of earthen monument. Although attendance at the Decoration Day was usually heavy and somewhat festive with families meeting to eat and recall former times, the cemetery itself was not the subject of serious efforts to clean, maintain and preserve. By the mid to late 1970s, the cemetery was covered in brush and sage grass and fire was often set to it to clear it. Of course, such grass fires also damaged cemetery stones and actually hindered efforts to preserve them.

Beginning in the 1980s and 1990s, serious efforts were made to raise money for the cemetery's upkeep. Thanks to the persistence and tireless effort of Richard Leath, a cemetery account was established and an endowment was built. Though small by some standards, its very existence is a testament to Mr. Leath's hard work and desire to see the cemetery perpetually maintained. Since that time, efforts by Ronald L. Talbott and the author have been made to make the cemetery grounds more maintainable and more uniform. The existence of the low-growing varieties of grass growing in much of the cemetery are there thanks to the time and energy of Ronald Talbott, who has taken enormous amounts of time sprigging and setting out various types of grasses which eventually overtook the high sage grass and other weeds in the cemetery. This activity has made mowing and maintenance of the cemetery much more efficient and effective.

17. The cemetery drive constructed in the late 1940s or early 1950s around Mount Carmel Cemetery was turned back to cemetery lawn space in 2008, and the driveway was covered with fill dirt and sewn with grass. It now comprises a portion of the cemetery lawn and is much more pleasing to the eye than the red gravel drive. The removal of the drive was in keeping with long-range plans to restore the cemetery grounds to its original purpose. Further, restoration of the space on the back side of the cemetery is in keeping with some type of recognition of that space as hallowed ground for those black citizens whose graves were so crudely disturbed and desecrated when the road was built after World War II.

Today, there is little wild or unpredictable about the cemetery grounds. Continual efforts are being made to preserve for the generations to come. The removal of the cemetery drive accomplished two goals. First, it returned to the cemetery a portion of the graveyard previously desecrated. Second, it made the cemetery a safer place to mourn and celebrate the lives of the dead interred therein. By 2008, the stewards of the cemetery had to deal with drug and criminal activities taking place on the grounds. As an isolated country cemetery, it was an ideal place for such activities. Cutting off the access to the west side of the cemetery forced individuals to park near the road. The goal of making the cemetery safe for legitimate visitors was accomplished.

Now the goal becomes the preservation of the aging and decaying tombstones of the nineteenth century. These stones are especially vulnerable to environmental factors that quickly erode the lettering of the stones. Responsible efforts are currently being made to effectively clean and preserve the stones. Maintenance and repair of damaged stones will allow the graves they mark to remain identifiable and not become another unmarked grave. Efforts at reclaiming previously unmarked but otherwise known graves began in the late 1990s. Since 2000, the author, with considerable cooperation from families and through careful research, has reclaimed more than thirty graves from near or future anonymity. These efforts remain active. Further, the marking of unknown but otherwise unmarked graves continues as well.

CHAPTER TWO

HISTORY OF THE
MOUNT CARMEL MEETING HOUSE

As to the meetinghouse at Mount Carmel, its history is spotty and incomplete at its very best. It has been said the original Mount Carmel meetinghouse stood in the northeast section of the present-day cemetery about where the graves of John Robert and Ollie Pearl McIntyre are today. In fact, members of that family once found an old square head nail while cleaning the graves of their parents. Whether or not it was from the old structure will never be known. The original building was probably a log structure that would have required wooden pegs in the construction process rather than iron nails. The author speculates whether the original structure might have been the original Matthew Ward dwelling. Although likely, it is also possible that Ward dismantled and moved his original structure. It may be that no structure existed until the frame meetinghouse was dismantled in the late 1930s and early 1940s.

The wood framed meetinghouse was a larger building than the present structure. The interior of the building was spacious and open. There was no ceiling of the modern sense. One could look up all the way to the rafters. The walls were beaded. There were a few old wooden pews in the structure for church services, funerals, and weddings. Apparently the building was used most frequently for Baptist or Wesleyan Methodist worship services. We know that from the 1860s through the 1880s, the meetinghouse was the site of Wesleyan Methodist meetings and religious

Sarah (McIntyre) Fowler and her nephew J.R. McIntyre stand by the doorway of the Mount Carmel Meetinghouse. This wooden building was later replaced by the present-day block structure.

services and that the Reverend Wilson A. McHolstead (1806–1891) preached here. We also know that during his lifetime, Elijah J. Hodges (1831–1913) practiced his vocation as a Primitive Baptist preacher here as well. There was also a Reverend Stansell, among others.[1] In the 1930s, the congregation was an older set of believers that included Pete and Lizzie Wharton, Newton Perry Talbott, and Lula (Womble) McIntyre. Occasionally, the believers of the black community used the meetinghouse for singings and preaching.

1. To avoid misunderstanding, the Reverend Stansell is not to be confused with Hallie Stanfill, a later preacher at Mount Carmel. They were two distinct individuals.

Mount Carmel Church in the late 1940s in front of the present-day block structure. Among the congregation are Charlie and Ludie Griffin, Pete Wharton (holding books) and Lizzie Wharton (front row, far right, wearing a hat), Mr. & Mrs. Hallie Stanfill, Ella King, and Nellie Sue Davis.

The congregation of Mount Carmel Church in the early 1960s. (Left to right) Front row: Callie Peddy, Melinda Lott, Nancy King, Mr. & Mrs. Albert Ross, unidentified girl. Back row: Mackie Lott, Max Lott, Lloyd & Lee Nell King, Mrs. Myrtle, and Mr. & Mrs.Hallie Stanfill.

One interesting story about the old meetinghouse involved a former slave known as "Coleman." Coleman lived with the John A. and Mary Roberta McIntyre family and as a slave had allegedly belonged to her mother, Isabella Jane Coleman. One night after dark, he had walked from the McIntyre place to the meetinghouse. Unbeknownst to Coleman, someone's sheep had gotten out and were loose inside the meetinghouse. He heard a racket and when he went to the window of the meetinghouse to investigate, he saw some vague white forms jumping over the pews. Being superstitious as many former slaves often were, Coleman took the vague forms of the sheep to be ghosts. He quickly took off back toward the McIntyre home and didn't stop running until he collapsed on the porch steps, exclaiming that ghosts were in the meetinghouse.[2]

Eventually, the large frame meetinghouse began to deteriorate. Someone removed the windows and doors from the structure and carried them away. Finally the time came to make a change. The decision was made to erect a new structure on roughly the same site. That meant tearing down the old structure. Henry Kirkpatrick bought the flooring and Zanie Brown bought the building itself. It was already leaning badly by the time it was actually demolished.

The present block meetinghouse was built in the late 1940s. Pete Wharton was the driving force behind its construction. However, it would not have been possible without the aid of so many donors who gladly contributed their time, expertise, and finances to the building of a new meetinghouse. In the 1980s, the building was used by the Mennonites for church services and a school. It was used as a church once again in the 1990s, but by 2000 it was largely in disuse. The current meetinghouse was badly in need of repair and renovation by 2013. Efforts began in January of that year to gut the building and begin substantial renovations to the structure. These efforts are projected to be completed by the spring of 2014. At that point, a functioning meetinghouse and interpretive display will be complete and functioning for the benefit of those

2. This story was related by various members of the McIntyre family during the period of the twentieth century. Siblings Lessie McIntyre, Roy McIntyre, Vivian McIntyre and Faye McIntyre Talbott told the story over and over during the decades of the twentieth century. Apparently, the story had been passed down from their father, John Robert McIntyre, who may have been a witness to Coleman's return to the home or heard it directly from witnesses in the family.

whose heritage is linked to Mount Carmel and for those who visit on the annual Decoration Day.

Elder Hallie Stanfill and his wife Myrtle (Peddy) Stanfill beside the front door of Mount Carmel Church in the early 1960s. Mr. Stanfill preached there for about 15 years from the late 1940s until the early 1960s.

The Mount Carmel Meetinghouse in 1993

CHAPTER THREE

❦

BIOGRAPHICAL SKETCHES OF
RESIDENTS OF MOUNT CARMEL CEMETERY

It is certainly possible to write an interesting sketch about almost any individual buried in the Mount Carmel Cemetery. However, the author has seen fit to provide sketches of certain of those buried in the cemetery whose overall accomplishments or activities were of a nature so as to warrant historical or other mention. Some of these men and women were involved in important events of their day and were, in many cases, respected far and wide during their lifetime. Others just were interesting individuals about whom information was available.

George W. Bulliner (1812–1873) & David A. Bulliner (1848–1874)
Participants and Victims of the "Bloody Williamson" Feud

The Bulliner family lived in the Anderson's Store region of north McNairy County. Those buried in the area are found in Mount Carmel

Tombstone of George W. Bulliner

Cemetery. The Bulliner family was listed by General Marcus J. Wright as being among the early families to have settled in the northern portion of the county. Those buried at Mount Carmel are marked as early as 1855. Perhaps there are earlier graves, but if so, they are unmarked.

Little is known of the Bulliner family, but there is one interesting incident regarding this family. More interestingly the event itself did not occur in McNairy County, but rather in the state of Illinois and the bodies were shipped home. The Bulliners had migrated from McNairy County, Tennessee to Williamson County, Illinois. This particular Illinois County became known as "Bloody Williamson" County. It was populated by natives of Tennessee, Kentucky, Virginia, and the Carolinas, families who were "hot-blooded, proud, obstinate, jealous of family honor, and quick to resent an insult."[1] During the second-half of the nineteenth century, feuds and violence were common in this Illinois county. The Bulliner family was headed by two brothers and had migrated from McNairy County in 1865 during the last year of the Civil War. The Bulliners settled south of Crainville, Illinois, in Williamson County.[2]

The Bulliner family became involved what would become known as the "Bloody Vendetta."[3] The feud began when several members of the family were playing cards in a tavern near Carbondale, Illinois with a

1. Paul M. Angle. *Bloody Williamson: A Chapter in American Lawlessness.* Chicago: University of Illinois Press, 1992, page 73.

2. *Id*, page 74.

3. *Id.*

man by the name of Felix "Field" Henderson, who hurled an insult at one of the Bulliners.[4] Henderson was badly beaten after calling one of the Bulliners "a damn lying son of a bitch" and following this incident, the Bulliners and the Hendersons became bitter enemies.[5]

According to historian Paul M. Angle, the Bulliner men were known as "honest, industrious and enterprising" and "big-boned, broad-shouldered, muscular, good-looking, and pleasant in manner, yet they could be most disagreeable to anyone who crossed them."[6] Like so many feuds in history, the one between these two families smoldered and gained momentum while awaiting an-

Tombstone of David A. Bulliner

other incident to occur. While the ill will between the Bulliners and the Hendersons mounted, a farmer named George W. Sisney and one of George W. Bulliner's sons became involved in a disagreement over a crop of oats.[7] The matter was heard in the courts and Sisney prevailed, but the two agreed to meet later and settle up their accounts.[8] Quickly, Sisney and Bulliner disagreed and the younger Bulliner man accused Sisney of perjury during the trial whereupon Sisney assaulted Bulliner, knocking him to the ground.[9]

4. *Id.*

5. *Id.*

6. *Id.*

7. *Id*, page 75.

8. *Id.*

9. *Id.*

George Bulliner and his sons took after Sisney and fired upon him as he ran across an open field, hitting him four times before he was able to reach shelter.[10] Each of the Bulliners involved were fined one hundred dollars each and Sisney brought a lawsuit against the Bulliner boys, which was settled out of court and never brought to trial.[11] Eventually a number of Williamson County families developed vendettas against one another and each one had allies as well as enemies in other families. These families involved included the Crains, Sisneys, Hendersons, and Bulliners.[12] The Crains and the Bulliners were allied against the Hendersons and the Sisneys.[13] Between 1872 and 1873, a number of brawls occurred in which various members of these four families were involved and in every resulting criminal case, the defendants were either acquitted or the prosecution was dropped.[14]

On December 12, 1873, sixty-one year old George W. Bulliner set out on horseback toward Carbondale, Illinois. Later in the day, neighbors found Bulliner lying dead by the side of the road with buckshot wounds in his back.[15] George Bulliner's body was brought back to north McNairy County and buried in Mount Carmel Cemetery near the grave of his mother, Rebecca Bulliner. A few months later, on or about March 29, 1874, two of George and Nancy Bulliner's sons were ambushed and wounded.[16] David A. Bulliner was twenty-five years old at the time and was mortally wounded.[17]

On the morning of March 30, 1874, death was closing in around young David Bulliner. According to Williamson County's first county historian, Milo Erwin, the scene of young Bulliner's death was as follows:

> The twilight shadow of death, cold and gray, came stealing
> on him. A supernatural lustre lighted up his eye, and illumi-
> nated the gathering darkness. At length his eyes closed, and

10. *Id.*
11. *Id.*
12. *Id.*
13. *Id.*
14. *Id.*
15. *Id.*
16. *Id.*
17. *Id.*

an expression of ineffable placidity settled on his pallid lips, and he was no more.[18]

Just prior to his death, Bulliner identified his assailant as Tom Russell, a man who had no connection to the vendettas but whose affections for a woman was spurned in favor of one of the Bulliner sons.[19] Again, a Bulliner was brought back to Tennessee to be buried in Mount Carmel Cemetery. Eventually, after Bulliner's brother, Monroe Bulliner, was unable to identify Tom Russell as the murderer, Tom Russell was acquitted.[20]

The feud would continue for decades and more Bulliners would be involved. It led to a series of feuds that fed upon themselves in Williamson County. The entire affair has been carefully documented by Illinois State Historian Paul M. Angle (1900–1975) in his work, *Bloody Williamson: A Chapter in American Lawlessness.*

Elijah James Hodges (1831–1913)
Union Army Officer, Minister, and Tennessee State Representative

Elijah James Hodges was born to Elisha Hodges and Millie (Ward) Hodges on the family farm near present-day Finger on May 18, 1831. Whether he was educated at home or obtained some formal schooling is not presently known, but Hodges was a well-read man of literary pursuits. He has been described as "an intellect and a great literary and Bible reader."[21]

Elijah and brother Horry enlisted in Company B of the First West Tennessee Cavalry, later known as the Sixth Tennessee Cavalry, on August 25, 1862, at Bethel Station.[22] On November 17, 1862, Hodges received a promotion to sergeant. Upon the death of William K.M. Breckinridge on October 15, 1863, he received a promotion to adjutant.[23] Hodges made the rank of first lieutenant on February 29, 1864. On May 5, 1864, Horry

18. *Id.*

19. *Id.*

20. *Id.*

21. Taken from Hodges' obituary in the *McNairy County Independent Appeal*, April 25, 1913.

22. Kevin D. McCann. *Hurst's Wurst: Colonel Fielding Hurst and the Sixth Tennessee United States Cavalry.* Ashland City, TN: Cardinal Press, 1997.

23. *Id.*

Hodges, the captain of Company B since its muster on August 25, 1862, died of smallpox in Helana, Arkansas. Upon his brother's death, Elijah James Hodges was elevated to captain, a rank he would hold until the war's end. He was discharged at Pulaski, Tennessee on July 26, 1865. It should be noted that Captain Elijah Hodges made an impressive sight leading his troops on the battlefield, as he stood six feet, six inches tall, an unusual height for a man in the nineteenth century.

Following the war, Hodges pursued a career as a politician, farmer, and preacher. He was elected to the Tennessee State House of Representatives on the Unionist ticket in 1867 and represented McNairy County in the Thirty-fifth General Assembly until 1869. He was also a well-known Primitive Baptist preacher, leading among others the congregation at Mount Carmel near his home.

Elijah married Nancy Jane Dodd on December 29, 1852, and to this union were born eleven children: Tabitha F. Hodges (December 28, 1854–August 29, 1855), Sarah Ann Hodges (August 24, 1857–July 27, 1858), John Hodges (January 27, 1862–April 18, 1862), Elizabeth Ellen Hodges Peeples (1860–1939), Mary Hodges Robertson (1866–1941), Horry Hodges (March 19, 1868–September 23, 1940), William Henry Hodges (September 19, 1869–November 16, 1941), Harmon E. Hodges (December 3, 1871–November 17, 1957), Rozetta Jane "Jennye" Hodges Scott (June 12, 1873–September 14, 1956), Maggie Hodges (March 27, 1876–October 30, 1955), and Harvey G. Hodges (March 17, 1878–September 1, 1922).[24]

Elijah often spoke at Union Army reunions and other events in his later years. More than a year prior to his death, he lost his eyesight, but according to his obituary, "everyday he was read to by some member of the family."[25] Elijah James Hodges died on April 21, 1913, at his home just east of the town of Finger and was buried in Mount Carmel Cemetery. Following the Captain's death, the remaining single Hodges' children, Horry, Henry, Harmon, Maggie, and Harvey, allegedly signed a

24. Of these eleven, several will be featured in biographical sketches in other portions of this work.

25. *McNairy County Independent Appeal*, April 25, 1913.

Captain Elijah J. Hodges of the Sixth Tennessee Cavalry and his tombstones

pact requiring each of them to remain single and to provide for their widowed mother and the family estate.[26]

Harmon E. Hodges (1871–1957)
McNairy County Surveyor, Farmer, and Educator

Harmon E. Hodges was born on December 3, 1871, in McNairy County, Tennessee. He was the next youngest of Captain Elijah James and Nancy Jane Dodd Hodges' sons. He was trained as an educator in his early years. He taught school for a period of time and taught at Finger and Lane's Academy. Eventually he became a surveyor and farmer. According to his family members, Harmon could grow some of the biggest hogs and he took great pride in his ability to garden and grow produce. His great-nephew, Jerry Wilson Smith, later an educator, once recalled that Harmon once declared to him, "Son, you'll never be farmer." Wilson also recalled that Harmon used a large basket with which to pick cotton rather than pull a common pick sack.

Harmon was heavily involved in the local agricultural societies and organizations of the day. He was quiet in nature like his brother, William Henry Hodges. He was known to be an industrious person who was also very thrifty. He served as the County Surveyor for McNairy County for several years. Harmon also helped to establish the Finger Cemetery by a simple act. Upon the death of Andrew J. Maness, one of Finger, Tennessee's leading spirits and entrepreneurs, in 1913, the decision was made to bury him on the land of James R. McIntyre. Harmon and Zanie Brown went to the knob on which Maness was to be buried and cleared the area of its blackberry vines in order to dig the grave. Like his siblings, Harmon continued to live on the old

Harmon E. Hodges as a young man

---

26. This has been passed down over the years by members of the family, family friends, and neighbors in the community.

Hodges farmstead long after the death of his parents. He never married. After the deaths of Horry and Henry in 1940 and 1941 respectively, he continued to live with his sister Maggie. He moved to Selmer after Maggie's death. He died on November 17, 1957, the last survivor of the children of Elijah James and Nancy Jane Dodd Hodges. His death closed a chapter on one of McNairy County's oldest and most respected families.

Professor Harvey G. Hodges (1878–1922)
Educator, Gospel Song Writer, and Satirist

Harvey G. Hodges could be described in so many ways. Harvey the amusing one might be appropriate after a quick perusal of his letters. Perhaps Harvey the passionate educator or Harvey the musical one could be utilized. Unfortunately, it seems that a most fitting term for Harvey is tragic and this is most unfortunate.

Harvey was born on the family farm near present-day Finger on March 17, 1878. He was the youngest child of Captain Elijah James and Nancy Jane Dodd Hodges. As such he was petted greatly by his older and adoring sisters, especially Maggie, his spinster sister.[27] As his brothers and sisters all did at some point in their lives, Harvey followed the path of the educators and sought his rewards in the field of teaching. According to the available accounts and records, Harvey taught in the county's public schools for over twenty years. Some of the schools where Harvey taught include Stantonville (1910) and Liberty Schoolhouse (1913). Certainly there were plenty of others, but

Harvey G. Hodges

27. This has long been told by members of the family and their neighbors and close friends.

due to the lack of adequate recordation, it is difficult to obtain a complete picture of Harvey's teaching career. It is known that in late 1920, Harvey became the principal of the Gravel Hill School, where he served until his death.

Harvey, like his brothers and sisters, was a man of immense talents and varying interests. A highly literate man of letters, he and his family possessed some of the great works of history and literature in their private home library. Yet one of his great loves was music. Instrumental in the success of the annual Singers' General Assembly, a large gathering of up to 20,000 attendees, Harvey found great spiritual solace and enjoyment in putting his strong religious beliefs into verse. He put to pen a wonderful gospel song, which he labeled "a sacred song," entitled *Traveling Home*. A verse from that song would eventually serve as Harvey's tombstone epitaph.

Harvey's surviving letters and newspaper contributions revealed that he had a comical touch and amusing side. He was a true wordsmith possessing the ability to turn a phrase. However, the great point of his life that was most discussed by those who recalled him was, most unfortunately, his death. Harvey's death has been cloaked in a shroud of mystery since its occurrence in 1922. Harvey and brother Henry both had been sickly off and on through the years. Many have stated the two suffered from tuberculosis, but this cannot be conclusively known. Regardless, according to the surviving newspaper accounts, Harvey was sick at the end of his life. According to his obituary, Harvey had to return home from his teaching at Gravel Hill School because of ill health brought on by an attack of influenza. The same account stated that Harvey "went home and while he rallied many times, he gradually grew worse until the end."[28]

The next line of Harvey's obituary is interesting and shows the close relationship between the older sister and the younger brother. Maggie Hodges was present "being constantly with him, her fidelity and gentleness soothing his last hours, during all of which he showed that masterful cheerfulness which was a part of his nature, and endured with the same patient nobility to the end."[29] However, what was the nature of Harvey's sickness and death? That may be hard to ever determine, for many different stories are told. It is known that Harvey was engaged

28. *McNairy County Independent Appeal*, September 8, 1922.

29. *Id.*

to a fellow teacher by the name of Ethel Plunk. Apparently the couple was very adamant in their desire to marry as both were past the average age of marriage with Harvey at the age of forty-four. Those who have any knowledge of the relationship have stated that Maggie was firm in her opposition to the proposed marriage. It was this disagreement between Maggie and her beloved younger brother that caused events to spiral out of control and lead to Harvey's physical demise.

According to local lore and even some members of the Hodges' family, all remaining Hodges' siblings signed a pact upon the death of their father, Captain Hodges, to remain

Tombstone of Harvey G. Hodges

unmarried and tend to their mother and the family home and estate until their respective deaths. Apparently Harvey intended to breach this agreement and Maggie held firm to her conviction that Harvey should abide by his word as per the agreement. It was additionally stated that Maggie was also opposed on political and familial grounds. The stories then hold that Harvey, in anger and pride, moved out of the family home and camped in a fallen treetop in the woods on the Hodges' farm. It was here that he was said to have developed either influenza or pneumonia. Regardless, Harvey died on September 1, 1922, and was buried next to his parents in Mount Carmel Cemetery with the Reverend Dewberry preaching and John R. Swaim and W.H. Wilson singing. As was earlier stated, Harvey wrote his own epitaph, a line from a song he had written earlier in life:

> *We're traveling on and seeking our own,*
> *To rest after toil, to know and be known,*
> *To scenes of delight, to peace and reward,*
> *To dwell with the saints who trusted the Lord.*

Maggie and Harvey shared an especially close relationship, probably much closer than between any other of the siblings. Harvey's obituary reveals a little about their closeness as it speaks of Maggie presence with Harvey near the end and certainly to the very tragic and sad end.

What truly became of Harvey Hodges may never be conclusively known. Perhaps he simply became sick and came home to die of natural causes as was reported in 1922. Perhaps his own pride and independence caused his eventual demise. Many tales have been told including some which were not very noble, but the truth remains that we may never truly know. Still, there has long been tale of a more ignoble end. According to some of the older citizens, it was accepted that Harvey had actually committed suicide over the emotional conflicts with his siblings regarding his unpopular marital engagement. According to the late L.E. Talbott, his father-in-law, John Robert McIntyre, a neighbor to the Hodges, was among the party called upon to look for Hodges in the woods around his house because he went missing. According to Talbott, McIntyre related that Hodges was found leaning against a tree and that he was found to have actually shot himself. Further, in a 1994 interview by the author with the late Clifford Young (then past 90 years of age), he stated unequivocally that Harvey committed suicide. Young said that he remembered the day well. Interestingly, the mortality records for the county show that he died of tuberculosis, not the influenza as reported in the local newspaper. Another local source, the late Hayes Hayre, also stated during to his lifetime that Hodges was believed to have committed suicide.

Professor Horry Hodges (1868–1940)
McNairy County Superintendent of Schools, Trustee, Circuit Court Clerk, Lawyer, Congressional Secretary, Educator, Writer, and Historian

It is almost impossible to know where to begin in the quest to write a brief biographical sketch of the late Professor Horry Hodges. Although his name is all but lost to the present generation, his was a name well-known and almost synonymous with higher learning, scholarship and oratory. He was indeed a true Renaissance Man. Few men ever graced the county with such a presence as Horry and yet, as with all mortal men, he has gone from the world. What may have sealed his fate in near certain anonymity was the fact that Horry, like all of his brothers and one of his sisters, never married and brought children into this world. Therefore, it was all but impossible for his great legacy to continue unfettered.

Perhaps the most effective way in which to present the life of this famed educator is to do so chronologically. Even this will be challenging, as Horry was quite active and often on the go, leaving little in the way of records. Most of the record of his professional and even personal activity comes to the present generation in the way of correspondence and newspaper accounts. To the average member of 21st century

Horry Hodges

American society examining the newspapers of yesteryear, Horry Hodges seems the greatest of oddities. Here in the early years of the twentieth century, we find a newspaper and hence an entire county keeping up with the wild and interesting life of an itinerate genius and scholar as he travels the country and the county teaching and enlightening the young. With the aid of wonderful sources, now let us look in on an interesting and fully lived life from long ago.

Horry Hodges began his life in the type of environment he could only have wished. The son of the very literate and highly intelligent Captain Elijah J. Hodges, Horry's exact birthplace is currently in question. Although originally thought to have been born on the family farm near present-day Finger, recent discoveries reveal funeral home records that list Horry's birthplace as Morgan County, Alabama.[30] How could this be? Captain Hodges was serving in the Tennessee House of Representatives from 1867 until 1869 in the state capitol city of Nashville. Family members have speculated that Mrs. Nancy Jane Dodd Hodges, Horry's

30. Funeral records from the old Gooch Funeral Home in Selmer, Tennessee, list both Horry's and Dr. Henry Hodges' birthplaces as Morgan County, Alabama, with the source for the information being their sister Maggie Hodges.

mother, may have gone to Alabama to reside with relatives. However, this cannot be confirmed.

Regardless of the place, Horry was born on March 19, 1868. He received his primary education in the Jackson District High School in Henderson, Tennessee.[31] Horry continued his studies there in Henderson at West Tennessee Christian College graduating with his A.B. in 1891 and his A.M. in 1893. Here he studied under such men as Arvy Glenn Freed and with such great minds as that of Nicholas Brodie Hardeman. Early in his life, Horry was involved with the Primitive Baptist Church, with which his father was associated for so long. On May 12–14, 1886, at the Sunday School Convention in Adamsville, convention president J.W. Purviance "stressed the fact that the present convention was a business meeting in which God-fearing men and women came together to do a great work" and appointed "a resolutions committee composed of Horry Hodges, Dr. G.W. Morris, and J.H. Scott."[32] According to the report, "Horry Hodges addressed the children's department, and was most successful in his efforts to arouse interest. He loved the children and they loved him as well."[33] This testifies to Horry's interest in church affairs and in the welfare of children, for at this time Horry was only eighteen years old.

Horry began teaching school in 1887, long before earning his degree, no impediment at that time. Teaching would forever remain first in his heart and ever-present on his mind. However, politics would always lurk in the background and occasionally lurch forward to the forefront of his life. In 1894, Horry was elected to the office of circuit court clerk of McNairy County and served in that position until 1898. During this term, Horry studied law and successfully sat for the bar, being admitted to the local bar in January 1901. In 1898, Horry was elected to another countywide office, that of superintendent of schools, defeating the incumbent superintendent Calvin Hamm. After two years in the office, Horry taught two years at Shiloh National Military Park.[34] In 1902, Horry was again an official of McNairy County, this time serv-

31. Judge John Allison. *Notable Men of Tennessee: Personal and Genealogical with Portraits.* Atlanta, GA: Southern Historical Association, 1905.

32. J.C. Taylor. *Historical Articles.* This work was compiled and privately published in 1992.

33. *Id.*

34. *Id.*

ing as county trustee. In this position, Horry served as the county's chief financial officer until 1908.

During this extensive period of public service, Horry apparently remained active in the field of education. According to *The Selmer Post*, Horry presented a paper at the Teachers' Institute at Gravel Hill entitled "The Student, What Is He?"[35] An article from *The Weekly Post* speaks of H. Hodges' intent to deliver a lecture at the night session of The Teachers' Institute at Gravel Hill in November 1903, entitled "A True Education."[36] After he stepped down as county trustee, Horry took a teaching position at Bethel Springs High School in September of 1908.

During this period of his career, Horry became active in the area as a public speaker, which would eventually establish him as the greatest orator McNairy County ever produced. The records establish that he was active in the organization and activities of several local Civil War reunions and groups. In 1909, Horry accepted a job as the organizer of the Improved Order of Red Men in Tupelo, Mississippi, a job for which he received a "handsome salary."[37]

In June 1911, Horry was appointed principal of the McNairy County High School. Sometime after this time, he moved west. However, before leaving, Horry taught a term of summer school for brother Harvey at Liberty in the summer of 1913. Afterwards, Horry made his way to Paul's Valley, Oklahoma, to seek a teaching position. He did better. By September, Horry was employed as both a teacher and an administrator. A 1913 letter to Colonel J.W. Purviance stated, "I am pleased here because I have a good position. We have 12 teachers and opened with 314 students. We now have more than 340. I teach 3½ hours each day and get out at 2:30 p.m."[38] Most probably Horry also taught in Oklahoma the following year. By 1915, Horry was back in McNairy County. From 1915 to 1916, he taught at Selmer High School. However, sometime in this period, he also taught in Cash, Arkansas, Lindsey, Oklahoma, and New Mexico. In this county, Horry taught at the Center Hill Academy and Acton at some point.

35. *The Selmer Post*, April 24, 1903.

36. *The Weekly Post*, November 13, 1903.

37. *The McNairy County Independent Appeal*, August 13, 1939. This item for 1909 was found in the "Thirty Years Ago" column.

38. *The McNairy County Independent Appeal*, September 12, 1913.

In 1920, politics again entered into Horry's mind and occupied his energies. Apparently he was offered the Republican party nomination for the United States House of Representatives, but he declined the offer and instead favored Lon Allen Scott of Savannah, Tennessee. That fall, Scott was elected and Horry went with him to Washington, D.C. to serve as his personal secretary. After beginning his new work, Horry wrote back home that he was "well pleased with his position as secretary for Congressman Lon A. Scott" and while gone was "known throughout Washington, D.C. for his great knowledge of history."[39] While in the nation's capitol, Horry had opportunities unlike any. He had access to one of the greatest and voluminous collections of works in the country, the Library of Congress. It was reputed that he spent much of his time researching and reading in the great library. In fact, when he prepared to return to Tennessee in 1922, he was quoted as saying, "you know, Lon, I hate to leave Washington, there are still a few books in that building that I haven't read."

Another event of great interest to Horry was the hearing of a case before the United States Supreme Court. The states of Texas and Oklahoma were involved in a boundary dispute, a dispute that eventually made its way to the highest court in the land. The state attorney general of Oklahoma happened to be Sargent Prentice Freeling, who was originally from McNairy Station, Tennessee. He was a personal friend of Horry's and invited him to witness the specter of a Supreme Court case. Whether Horry, a licensed attorney, was asked to sit in as assistant counsel or in some other official capacity that would justify his presence as required by Supreme Court rules is not known. Freeling grew up in McNairy Station and attended Southwest Baptist University (now Union University) and later Harvard Law School. Freeling won the case for Oklahoma, defeating Texas and its two attorneys, one of whom was a former United States Attorney General.

In the fall of 1922, Lon Scott was defeated after just one term by Captain Gordon Browning of Huntington. After Horry came home to McNairy County, he was in great demand as a speaker. He traveled throughout the area speaking on matters of politics, religion and history. On many occasions, Horry, as the invited guest, would entertain and inform crowds of hundreds and even thousands at festivals, barbecues,

39. *The McNairy County Independent Appeal,* March 25, 1921, and September 27, 1940.

reunions, decoration days and meetings. Often Horry was called upon to speak at the opening or closing of schools and when called upon to make an impromptu speech, he would deliver wonderful talks due to his well-informed nature. In regards to Horry's depth and capacity of mind, it is said that upon hearing a verse of Scripture, he is said to have had the ability to quote the verse before it and the verse that followed.

After his stint as personal secretary to Congressman Scott ended, Horry did not abstain from politics for very long. On Saturday, April 19, 1924, the Seventh District Congressional Convention met in Jackson and nominated Horry for the U.S. House of Representatives. After an apparently quiet campaign, Horry was defeated in the general election by the incumbent Congressman Gordon Browning. It has been stated by family members that Horry was a very reluctant candidate, agreeing to run only out of loyalty to his party, the Republican party.

Horry continued to teach school after 1924 and spent some of his time and energy researching and writing history. He wrote many articles for various newspapers on the subject of history. Many of his writings dealt with state and local politics and history. As a historian, Horry was known throughout the state and considered one of Tennessee's foremost historians.[40] At the time of his death, Horry had been working on a book-length history of McNairy County, but died before he could complete the task.[41] Horry's notes and research have apparently disappeared. Due to Horry's persistence and dedication, his account of the naming of the town of Finger is the only recorded contemporary account of the event.

Following the 1924 general election, Horry returned immediately to his beloved labor, that of teaching. In August of 1924, he had been present for the opening of the Selmer school, but in September he officially returned. Taking the position of principal at Adamsville High School, the newspaper reported "Horry has gone back to his first love, in teaching lines. He assumes the principalship of the Adamsville school, a school with which he was identified in the years that are gone. The kind of teachers of which Mr. Hodges is a splendid example has always done a wonderful lot of good in this and other counties in the state, and we predict that the Adamsville school under his management and leadership will take a prominent part in the educational affairs of the county. He

40. *The McNairy County Independent Appeal*, September 27, 1940.

41. Taylor, *Historical Articles*

knows every angle of the great profession, and is thoroughly grounded and prepared in all things that belong to the life of the teacher."[42]

In 1926, Horry again heeded "the call of the wild and returned to the ranks of the pedagogues" when he was named the principal of the Enville High School.[43] Horry continued to teach in the schools of the county for the next decade as well as engage in other activities and events of an educational or cultural nature. In 1934, Horry was invited to speak at Freed-Hardeman College, the successor to West Tennessee Christian College. This was certainly at the invitation of the president of the school, Professor Nicholas Brodie Hardeman, an old and warm friend of Horry's. The following was a report of that speech:

> NOTED EDUCATOR HIGHLY HONORED: Prof. Horry Hodges, one of the foremost educators in the state, accepted an invitation to deliver a lecture at the summer school of the Freed-Hardeman College on the evening of Tuesday, June 26, 1934. He responded in a way that captivated the large attendance of students and visitors. His subject was "American History," with which none is more familiar.[44]

Such events and invitations were common in the life of Horry Hodges, as he enjoyed a widespread reputation for his oratory and his status as a Renaissance man.

Horry was also involved in a number of other activities besides teaching and speaking. He was involved in the Annual Singers General Assembly, a singing convention whose name is owed to the imagination and mind of Horry Hodges himself.[45] Until 1940, Horry never missed a meeting of the association, and upon his death, special songs were dedicated by the estimated 21,000 in attendance at the 22nd annual convention in observance of his death.

At the time of his death, Horry was an instructor in history and foreign languages at the Michie High School. His health was beginning to

42. *The McNairy County Independent Appeal*, September 12, 1924.

43. *Id.*, February 12, 1926.

44. *Id.*, dated from 1934 and contained in a scrapbook belonging to Elizabeth "Bessie" Abernathy Bigger (1875–1941).

45. *The McNairy County Independent Appeal*, September 27, 1940.

Tombstone of Horry Hodges and his brother Dr. William Henry Hodges

fail two months before his death, and some have stated they believe he may have suffered from cancer. Horry had made either a religious conversion in his life or he finally just settled on his own religious path. Although the son of a well-known Primitive Baptist preacher, Horry was a member of the Christian Church as early as 1905. This was about the time of the great decisive split in the Churches of Christ over the use of instrumental music in worship. Regardless, Horry's old friends, Judge J.C. Houston, and Nicholas B. Hardeman, conducted the services. Horry was buried in Mount Carmel Cemetery. He was an active member of the Republican Party, a member of the Royal Arch Masons, and had been chancellor commander of the local lodge of the Knights of Pythias and a member of Woodmen of the World.

William Henry Hodges, M.D. (1869–1941)
Educator and Physician

Dr. William Henry Hodges was born into a family of high intelligence, boundless ingenuity, and a level of curiosity which if satisfied could very well be quite voluminous. The son of Captain Elijah James Hodges, a farmer, politician, preacher, and soldier, and Nancy Jane (Dodd) Hodges,

he was born on September 19, 1869. According to his sister Maggie
Hodges, he and brother Horry were born in Morgan County, Alabama.
Regardless of his birthplace, Henry was raised on the Hodges' family
farm outside of present-day Finger. Like his brothers and sisters, he was
surrounded by books and the love of learning was instilled in him by his
father, a man of literary pursuits. After attending the district schools in
Henderson, Henry taught school for a period before deciding to follow
a career in medicine.[46]

In 1898, Henry graduated from the University of Nashville Medical School.[47] Henry immediately began practicing medicine actively and
was soon recognized for his ability and skill as a medical professional. A
newspaper quote previously cited again evidences Henry's professional
reputation:

> Dr. Henry Hodges, of McNairy, has come to be a frequent
> professional visitor in Selmer and sometimes talks of locating
> here. Dr. Hodges is a physician of more than ordinary attain-
> ments for his age, and, with close application, he is destined
> to rank high in his profession.[48]

His expertise in the field of anatomy, physiology and medicine was
such that he was consulted by his peers, by patients from all over the
countryside, and even by the court in special cases where expert opinion
testimony was required.

Henry was a quiet man whose nature was reserved and contemplative.
He was remembered by many for sitting in his library, quietly reading
and studying works of literature, history, science, religion and medicine.
However, there was another side to the good doctor, much like there is
to any individual. He had a light and humorous side like anyone else
and most likely a playful side. The following letter from W.H. Mills, the

---

46. It is not currently known when Doctor Hodges attended college and pursued his under-
graduate degree, but he probably attended West Tennessee Christian College were Horry attended.

47. This school is now the Vanderbilt University Medical School in Nashville, Tennessee.

48. *The Weekly Post*, November 13, 1903.

president of *The National Association of Railway Agents*, of Norwalk, Ohio, illustrates the more colorful self which Henry apparently possessed.[49]

Norwalk, Ohio
Dec. 11th, 1902.

Friend Doc,

I think I wrote to you last and as yet I have never read any reply, what has become of you? Have you got married to that little girl with the straw hat you told me about, or have you joined the Church and quit drinking? How is everyone at McNairy and what has become of my side partner "Gould?" He said he was going to write to me but I have never received his letter yet. How is our friend Mrs. Franklin, and John and the Miss Franklin; also the good looking Station Agent? How is Mrs. Sheffield? Give them all my regards. How is the quail crop this year, are you going to have many of them? I am going to St. Louis next month on business but hardly think I will be able to get down that far this winter. I would like very much to come down and have a time with you and the other boys. How is Joe Rouse? Is he still on the turf?

You had better meet me in St. Louis and I will give you a time that you will never forget. How many puppies have you sold for me? I am going to raise a car load or two and would like to get you to act as agent for me in selling them. "That little old dog" of mine is still on the turf and can beat the "ASS" off of any of the rest around here finding quail. I have been troubled with falling of the Womb and can't walk so far as I could. Can you send me a remedy for the trouble? Let me hear from you and all about McNairy and what has been going on

49. The letter has a type of earthy character to it and suggests that Dr. Henry Hodges, like many younger men, knew how to have a good time. The letter discusses what many such letters among men of that period did, weather, hunting, dogs and women and not in that particular order. Certainly we can see that Dr. Hodges was more than just a bookworm with an insatiable appetite for books and academic pursuits. One interesting note regards Mills' tongue in cheek mention of joining the church. When speaking with members of the family and those who were well-acquainted with them, no one seems to have known Dr. Hodges' religious preference. No reference was made in his obituary as to his religious beliefs, but only that his services were held at the Finger Church of Christ.

down there since I was there last winter; also how the quail are
and if there is any good hunting there this year. Something
might turn up that we might run down and make you a call.
What kind of weather are you having? It has been very cold
here but is some warmer now but I do not think it will last
long. Ask Gould if he wants us to come down and if he will
go hunting with me if I will come. Tell him I will shoot him
some more rabbits. Herb was hanged for horse stealing and
White is in jail for robbing chicken roosts and I have joined
the Salvation Army. So you will have to be careful how you
act if I come. Let me hear from you at once.

With kind regards to all of the McNairy friends, I am,

> Yours Truly,
> W.H. Mills

p.s. I know some good stories which I will tell you when I
see you, and soon.

Henry's range of interests went far beyond that of science or medicine. He was a true lover of history. Many were the times that Horry
and Henry made the short trip to Squire James Simpson "Simp" Lain's
humble home to discuss the great events of old and their many implica-
tions. History was a favorite subject. One young man was granted permission to use the Hodges' private library to research a historical debate.
The debate pitted this young man as Ulysses S. Grant and a classmate as
Robert E. Lee and thus "Grant" was permitted to use the family library
for research purposes. Henry looked up from his own studies and in-
structed the young man, "Tell them Grant commanded more men that
Napoleon or Caesar and was never driven from the field."[50]

Many of the older residents of north McNairy County do not remember Henry practicing medicine actively, but rather remember him for the
advisory role he appeared to play when consulting with other physicians.
In fact, many local doctors in the area called upon Henry's expertise and
seemingly boundless knowledge of the body and medicine to supplement
their own reservoir and to assist them in making crucial medical deter-
minations. However, he was actively engaged in the practice from 1898

50. The young "Grant" was future teacher and politician Lloyd Harris and the student "Lee"
was Crolin Plunk, a classmate and future attorney.

until 1937 or 1938. According to one member of the family, Henry was employed full-time as doctor at Western State Mental Asylum from 1922 until 1938. This has been confirmed by others.[51]

Off and on through the years, Henry was afflicted with pain and sickness. The exact problem or cause remains a mystery. Again, some have stated that his problem, as with Harvey, was tuberculosis, but this cannot be proven. Regardless, ill health forced him to retire in the late 1930's. His physical health weakened, but not his mind. His drive to learn and share with others continued. One gentleman stated that an afternoon ride

Dr. William Henry Hodges

with "old Doc Hodges" could teach you more than you had ever learned in your life otherwise.[52] The author of the *Cyclone Bill* column wrote about all four Hodges' brothers when commenting upon Henry's death: "I never met any one of these four boys and talked with them any length of time that I didn't learn something that I didn't know before."[53] On November 16, 1941, a Sunday afternoon, Dr. William Henry Hodges died at his family home after a prolonged illness. Henry's funeral services were held at the Finger church of Christ on Monday afternoon, November 17, 1941, with a Brother Cox and Judge J.C. Houston officiating. Henry

51. Jerry Wilson Smith, a grandson of Mary Hodges Robertson, sister to Dr. William Henry Hodges, stated in a July 1996 interview at his home in Friendship, Tennessee, that when he spent summers there in the 1920s and 1930s, Henry was employed at the asylum. He stated that Henry caught the train to Bolivar on Monday mornings and came back to Finger on Friday afternoons. Ben Davidson, great-grandson of Bettie Hodges Peeples, also a sister of Dr. Hodges', says he believes he has heard the same.

52. Interview with Guy Brown of Finger, Tennessee, in 1995.

53. *McNairy County Independent Appeal*, November 21, 1941.

was laid to rest beside his brother Horry in the old burying grounds of Mount Carmel Cemetery.

Hugh Kerby (1821–1870)
Postmaster, Farmer, and First White Child Born in McNairy County

Hugh Kerby was a true pioneer child. According to all available sources, he was born to Francis and Nancy Sparks Kerby, in 1821 in the vicinity of Mount Carmel Cemetery. For a time, Hugh served as the postmaster of the Huggins Creek Post Office. He came to the post on June 7, 1854, succeeding James Wilson. However, the post office was discontinued on October 24, 1854. He married Martha Jane Hendrix, the daughter of Richard Ivy Hendrix and Rebecca Cherry Hendrix. Hugh and Martha had two children, Nancy E. Kerby Lain and Alonzo Kerby. At Hugh's death in 1870, he was buried in Mount Carmel Cemetery. In the 1950s, a substantial monument was erected at Mount Carmel to Hugh's memory. The inscription on that stone reads as follows:

> First White Child
> Born in McNairy Co.
> HUGH KERBY
> 1821–1870
> In Memory Of Hugh Kerby Born Near
> The Spot Where Here He Is Buried
> The First White Child Born In The Land
> Which In 1823 Became McNairy County
> This Monument Is Erected By A Greatful [sic]
> People In Honor Of A Child Of
> The Wilderness Son Of The Old
> Frontier Who With Others Of His Era
> Built For Us All A Citadel Of Liberty
> In A Beautiful Land

Francis Kerby settled on 42 acres on the banks of Hugganses Creek, now known as Huggins Creek. Although the deed was not registered until 1823, when the county was actually formed, it is likely that Hugh Kerby was born on this farm. According to his tombstone Hugh Kerby

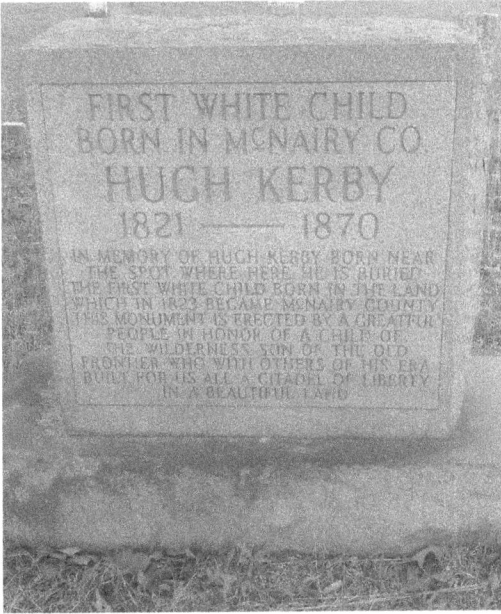

Tombstone of Hugh Kerby

was born near Mount Carmel hill, and it must be remembered that Mount Carmel is the high point in the terrain looking over Huggins Creek below. Interestingly, Frances Kerby's deed is the second deed to be recorded in McNairy County.

James Simpson "Simp" Lain (1845–1932)
McNairy County Magistrate, Educator, and Farmer

James Simpson "Simp" Lain was born on December 2, 1845, to Thomas and Jane A. Lain. Little is known regarding his early life. When the battle of Shiloh broke out on April 6, 1862, Simp was a young single man living and working on the farm. One man who remembered Lain as an old man recalled the old man saying he stood behind his barn on a hill and listened to the guns at Shiloh. The great battery of General Daniel Ruggles of the Confederacy was sixty-two guns strong and readily heard so far from the Tennessee River. Others remembered being down on Tar Creek in north McNairy County and seeing the water shimmer from the vibrations of the distant guns.

Tombstone of James Simpson Lain

Following the war, Lain chose a career as a schoolteacher. He was teaching as early as the 1870s and was the founder of Lain's Academy. Lain taught for several years and served as a member of the McNairy County Quarterly Court for a number of decades. It was on that body that he made many important votes, including voting to remove the county seat of McNairy County from Purdy. Lain was known during his day for the large number of people he joined in marriage.

Lain married Nancy E. Kirby (Kerby) September 16, 1866, with Justice of the Peace W.M. Crow officiating. They had four daughters and one son. Hugh M. Lain was born on October 29, 1867, and died on June 30, 1868. Arminta Lain was born on January 27, 1878, and died on August 6, 1889. Maudie Lain was born on August 10, 1886, and died on March 23, 1911. Jennie Lain was born on June 19, 1869, and married A. Kennel Tedford on November 24, 1885, with William Barney Malone officiating. Jennie died on September 27, 1919. These four were buried in Mount Carmel Cemetery close to Simp and Nancy Lain. Finally, Minta Pauline Lain was married to J.H. Leath.

On May 29, 1932, James Simpson Lain passed away and was buried in Mount Carmel Cemetery. Nancy E. Kirby Lain died on November 10, 1935, and was buried next to her husband.

Jacob Lowrance (1803–1882)
McNairy County Magistrate and County Trustee

The simple slab of limestone marking the silent earthen tomb of Jacob Lowrance says so little about the life its occupant lived. To stand before this thin slab one can learn only the name and dates, but there is so much more to know about this man. Jacob Lowrance began this life on April 20, 1803, twenty years before the formation of McNairy County. He was the son of Abram Lorance, one of the earliest settlers in the county, who settled in the north end of the county in 1824. Jacob married Susana Gage, the daughter of Aaron Gage. Gage was himself a veteran of the Revolutionary War who also had settled in the county around 1824. Susana was born on October 14, 1814. She and Jacob had at least three children: Elizabeth Lowrance, David Marion Lowrance, and John M. Lowrance.[54] Elizabeth was born between 1830 and 1840 and married a Tedford. David Marion Lowrance was born in February of 1834. John M. Lowrance, born in 1836, married Harriet E. Putman on January 27, 1867. John and Harriet had three children by 1870: David M. Lowrance, born in 1868 or 1869, and twins William S. Lowrance and Martin E. Lowrance, born in 1869 or 1870. Susana died on April 19, 1837.

As to the identity of a fourth child of Jacob and Susana, there is some disagreement and controversy. Buried next to Jacob in Mount Carmel Cemetery is Mary Covey.[55] Some sources have said Mary is the daughter of Jacob and Susana. Others have said she was the second wife of Jacob. Regardless, this is what we know of her. Mary, who was born on January 6, 1833, and died on January 24, 1893, was married Charles B. Covey (1824–1862), who served in Company B of the U.S. Sixth Tennessee Cavalry during the War Between the States. Covey died on November 22, 1862 and was buried in Mount Carmel Cemetery. The couple had four children: Fineti Covey, born in 1849; Henry H. Covey, born in 1856; Martha A. Covey, born in 1858; and Susan L. Covey, born in 1860. From there nothing is really definitely known about Mary's activities or relationships. The rest may be purely speculation at this point.

54. The information regarding these three children comes from *The History of the Lowrance Family* compiled by Marie F. Whitehead.

55. In Naylor and Talbott's *Fingerprints*, Mary Covey was identified as the second wife of Jacob Lowrance, based upon existing written records and sources.

Tombstone of Jacob Lowrance

In 1870, the Federal Census records that Mary was living with Jacob Lowrance and his son David M. Lowrance, along with her children. However, this should not be taken as evidence that Mary and Jacob were unrelated and had been married, for there is no marriage record of such a union in existence. It is therefore more likely that Mary was indeed the child of Jacob and Susana Lowrance and that she moved back into the house with her father upon the death of her husband in 1862. There is a child buried next to Jacob and Mary in Mount Carmel Cemetery by the name of John L. Lowrance (March 28, 1872–November 9, 1873) but this may very well be the child of either John or David Lowrance, the sons of Jacob.

Jacob Lowrance served in a number of capacities in county and local government during his years. He served on the McNairy County Quarterly Court a number of years including 1870 to 1876. He also served as McNairy County Trustee, only the fifth man in the county's history to hold that position. In regards to occupations, Jacob was also a grocer and merchant. He was also a member of the Freemasons. Jacob died on August 11, 1882.

If one were to visit the graves of this family at Mount Carmel they would find a seemingly peculiar sight, in that the graves are located in different parts of the cemetery. There is a simple explanation for this. When Susana died early in 1837, the cemetery at Mount Carmel was still relatively small and concentrated in the center portion of the present cemetery. As the years passed the circle of graves grew wider and larger. Eventually there was little or no room for some relatives to be buried next to those who were now long dead. The dates of the graves of Susana in

1837 and Jacob in 1882 give some idea of the years that passed and the graves that were established.

James Mason (1804–1880)
Farmer and Grandfather of Poet and Writer John Mason

The first of the Mason family to settle in north McNairy County was James Mason. James was born on July 1, 1804, in central North Carolina, near Fayetteville. He remained there until he was thirty-eight years old. He became involved in a quarrel with his father, Foster Mason, and traveled to West Tennessee on horseback. Unfortunately, the father and son never reconciled. According to Mason's grandson, John, he rambled across West Tennessee a year or two before buying 127 acres in north McNairy County from his brother Rufe Mason. According to John Mason, "there were a few acres cleared and a one-room cabin on the place Grandfather bought; maybe a side-room also, I remember seeing the skeleton walls of this old primitive building where my father and two or three of his brothers and sisters were born. Some years later my grandfather built a story and half house of heavy hews of logs on higher ground a hundred yards to the west."[56]

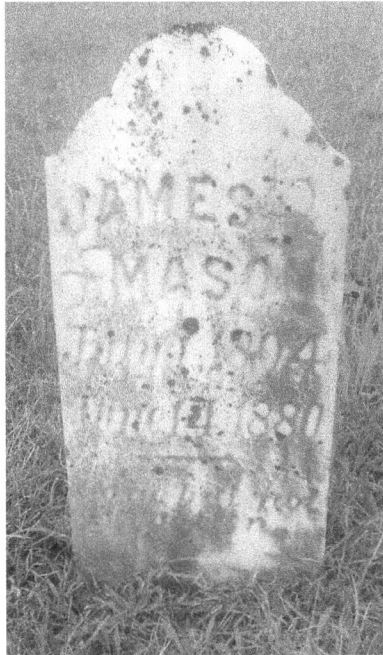

Tombstone of James Mason

James Mason married Margaret Priscilla Patterson in 1834. She was the daughter of Wilson and Charity Patterson, who came from the Greensboro, North Carolina area. The couple had at least six children. John Mason described his grandparents' physical features and personality traits. James Mason was a tall man for the times, six foot-two inches tall. He was "big-boned, lean and muscular; mentally alert; out-spoken, a

56. Ruth Helen Neimann. *The Glory of a Common Man: A Biography*. Privately published, 1976.

square-shooter; jovial, witty and at times sarcastic." Priscilla was rather short with a "dumpy build, brown eyes, and a great talker." According to the grandson, she was an excellent storyteller. James passed away on June 14, 1880, and was interred at Mount Carmel. Priscilla, who was born on January 13, 1814, died on July 20, 1888, and was buried next to her husband.

William Mason was born in 1835, the oldest of the children of James and Priscilla Mason. He married Sarah C. Floyd on July 15, 1866. The couple was married by the Reverend Wilson A. McHolstead, who is buried next to Mason's parents at Mount Carmel. William and Sarah were quiet natured people. According to their son, John Mason, Sarah could read and write and knew the fundamental operations of arithmetic, but she usually read only for an hour or so each Sunday. William was an intelligent man with an inquiring mind and an interest in certain types of literature. He was a farmer and occasional school teacher.

Their son, John, was born on August 9, 1867, in an old two-room frame house in the "southwest corner" of present-day Finger. According to John, the family moved one mile southwest to a farm known as the "Branch Place." According to John, the family's house was located close to a branch which drained several farms from both east and west before emptying its contents into Huggins Creek. John later migrated to the Indian Territory, which now comprises the state of Oklahoma. It was here that John married Etta Darrow on October 13, 1895. Over the years, John spent much time in reading, writing, and reflecting. He eventually published two books of poems, *Traditional Poems* and *Down to Earth Poems*. Following his death, his daughter completed and published his autobiography, *The Glory of a Common Man*. Shortly before his death, Oklahoma Governor Dewey Bartlett bestowed upon John the title of Honorary Oklahoma Ambassador because of his cultural contributions to Oklahoma. John Mason died on March 21, 1968, at more than one hundred years of age.

The Reverend Wilson A. McHolstead (1806–1891)
Respected Wesleyan Methodist Minister

Wilson A. McHolstead was born in North Carolina on November 11, 1806. He later came to McNairy County, but the exact year of his arrival is unknown. At what point he decided to turn his energies toward the ministry is unknown, but he became one of the most influential preachers of the Tennessee conference of the Wesleyan Church. He eventually served as president and secretary of the conference. In 1882, McHolstead served as secretary for the conference, the same year that another prominent McNairy County minister, F.M. Cude, served as president. An article from the *American Wesleyan* stated the following regarding McHolstead, "Brother McHolstead is a veteran in this Conference. He is seventy-five years of age, and he made a report which should fire the hearts of younger men to accomplish great things for Christ. He reported the largest salary of any man

*Tombstone of
Rev. Wilson A. McHolstead*

in the Conference, which was nineteen dollars and thirty cents. Part of this amount was actually paid over to him during the year, and the rest had been subscribed, and the account was thought to be good. This aged soldier of the cross living on 'borrowed time' said: 'I have preached seventy-one sermons and traveled seven hundred miles this year.' A good many miles on a small amount of money."[57]

McHolstead was married at least twice. His wife Elizabeth S. McHolstead is buried next to him in Mount Carmel Cemetery. However, there is the possibility that she is not his first wife and if she was, it was a late first marriage. In McNairy County's marriage records is a record of a marriage between a W.A. McHolstead and an E.S. Henderson on January 12, 1871. This may very well be Brother McHolstead. If so, he was sixty-five years old at the time and Elizabeth was sixty-two. Certainly, this couple had no children. Following her death in 1886, McHolstead

---

57. *American Wesleyan*, November 8, 1881. This excerpt was sent to the author in a letter from Donna Watson, Assistant Director of the Archives and Historical Library, International Center, The Wesleyan Church, Indianapolis, Indiana, on June 30, 1994.

married again, this time to Mary M. Yarbrough. The marriage ceremony took place on August 9, 1887, with Elijah J. Hodges officiating. Whether or not McHolstead had any children is not currently known. McHolstead passed away on March 23, 1891, at the age of eighty-four.

John Absalom McIntyre (1848–1897)
Farmer and Businessman

John Absalom McIntyre came from a long line of hardy people and was made much from the same grain as his forefathers, being very interested in both advancing the community and gaining a substantial estate through the virtues of hard work and thrift. He was born to Robert Thompson and Sarah Jane (Weaver) McIntyre on April 27, 1848. During the War Between the States, he saw his brother go off to war and never return. His father was a strong Unionist leader in north McNairy County and ardent foe of secession and the Southern cause. At that time, the local Confederate forces were conscripting young men into service, many of them against their will. Perhaps he thought the same fate might befall him, as he was put on the Mobile and Ohio train bound northward and eventually to a Union munitions/powder factory in Illinois. It was here he spent the war, most likely in Nashville, Illinois where his future mother-in-law and neighbor, Isabella Jane Coleman was residing at the time.

After the war, he farmed with his father and family in and around present-day Finger. Apparently he was a very ambitious young man as his personal holdings grew rapidly during the years 1880 to 1897.

John Absalom McIntyre

He acquired over a thousand acres in north McNairy County on just one farm. He also had other land holdings including a farm at Mount Peter and other lots and properties near his farm. It has been passed down that at one time, McIntyre's thousand acre-plus farm was completely enclosed by a split-rail chestnut fence. The late Hayes Hayre remembered the existence of an old split rail fence running near an old road on his father's place, which actually would have been a boundary for McIntyre's farm. He also had interests in the mercantile and retail business in the small settlement then becoming known as Finger, Tennessee.

McIntyre married Mary Roberta "Robertie" Coleman, the daughter of John and Isabel Jane Coleman, on March 18, 1880. The couple had a number of children including Zenar McIntyre, W. Adrian McIntyre, Zelphia Roberta (McIntyre) Sanders Whitt, Sarah (McIntyre) Whitt Fowler, John Robert McIntyre, and Ulysses Hubert McIntyre. Like his father, he was a strong Republican in his politics, a member of the Church of Christ, and a brother of the Free and Accepted Masons. He became sick with skin cancer after a spot appeared on his arm. In those early days when no significant treatment existed but major surgery, he soon withered. On the evening of November 6, 1897, lying in his bed, McIntyre told his eldest son, Adrian, to go feed the horses and tend to the barn chores. Shortly after sending him along, John Absalom McIntyre breathed his last and expired leaving a wife and six children, one of whom was only a few months old. McIntyre was buried in Mount Carmel Cemetery.

James Robert McIntyre (1849–1921)
Farmer, Co-Founder of Home Banking Company, and Developer of the Town of Finger

James "Jim" Robert McIntyre was the son of Robert Thompson McIntyre and Sarah Jane (Weaver) McIntyre and the brother of John Absalom McIntyre. He was born on November 29, 1849, in north McNairy County near present-day Finger. He married Margaret Rebecca Beene, the daughter of Allen Louis Beene and Mary Jane (Gordon) Beene, on December 28, 1870. Jim and Rebecca had eleven children and gained much prosperity during their marriage. Their children were Robert Allen McIntyre, B.A. McIntyre, Levi Benton McIntyre, Virgie McIntyre,

James Robert McIntyre and his wife Fannie E. (Carroll) McIntyre

Isaac T. McIntyre, John J. McIntyre, Callie McIntyre James, William Samuel McIntyre, Mary McIntyre Smith, an unnamed infant, and Henry McIntyre.

Tombstone of James R. McIntyre

As the years passed, Jim prospered in his land dealings and was involved in a number of ventures and businesses. He was part owner of McIntyre, James, and Company, a general merchandise company. He was on the board of directors of the Bank of Finger and on the first board of directors of Home Banking Company. As mentioned earlier, he sold the lots there in town to those who would eventually build homes and businesses. All of the lots there in Finger originally belonged to Jim McIntyre. He was also actively involved in the Finger Church of Christ. The original meeting place of the congregation was the old Possum Trot Schoolhouse, which Jim provided, and he served as one of the first elders of the congregation. The congregation eventually moved to a building built in large part by Jim on land he donated. The church continues to meet on that site today.

Rebecca passed away on November 16, 1904, and was buried in the Mount Carmel Cemetery. Following Rebecca's death, Jim eventually married Miss Fannie E. Carroll on March 24, 1907. Five children were born to this union: Ruth McIntyre Moore, Alice (McIntyre) McCaskill, Wilma (McIntyre) Sharpe, Rachel McIntyre, and Carroll McIntyre. In his old age, Jim remained active in civic and social affairs. He was member of the International Order of the Odd Fellows and the Free and Accepted Masons. Jim also donated the land for the Finger School and the Finger Cemetery. He first donated land for the cemetery in 1913 and then donated additional property in 1921 just two weeks before his death. Jim McIntyre died December 30, 1921, and was buried in the Mount Carmel Cemetery with Brother N.B. Hardeman officiating.

Robert Thompson McIntyre (1814–1902)
McNairy County Magistrate, First Presiding Justice of the McNairy County Quarterly Court, Operator of McIntyre's Mill, and Namesake of McIntyre's Switch Settlement

Robert Thompson McIntyre was born in Mecklenburg County, North Carolina, near Charlotte, on May 28, 1814. The son of Isaac and Elizabeth Thompson McIntyre, he was not far removed from the generations of the glorious days of the American Revolutionary War. His grandfather, John McIntyre Jr., was a soldier in the Continental Army, serving in South Carolina. His father was present as a boy when his own grandfather, John McIntyre Sr., and a group of neighbors and friends defeated a group of scavenging British troops under the command of Lord Charles Cornwallis. With the help of a colony of bees, the troops were successfully routed and the story of the "bees and the bullets" grew into the legend of the hornet's nest surrounding Charlotte.

Robert's father, Isaac, died while the children were young. After his burial in the old Hopewell Presbyterian Cemetery with so many ancestors, his widow Elizabeth struggled to continue. After some years, Elizabeth and her four sons and a daughter moved to north McNairy County in 1833. Surely the experience must have been daunting for a poor widow with five children making such a move completely on her own. Once in the present-day area of Finger, Robert, his mother, and his brother William Cogbourne McIntyre remained while his brothers moved on to other areas.

Like many of his generation in a relatively newly settled region, Robert was dependent upon himself to make life a success. He was married to Sarah Jane Weaver, the daughter of Absolom Weaver, another early settler. To this union were born seven children: Antione Jane Stewart, Sarah Elizabeth Massey, Isaac T. McIntyre, Amanda Dickey, James Robert McIntyre, John Absalom McIntyre, and Nancy Caroline McIntyre. A number of prominent and hardworking people would descend from these various lines. Some of Robert's grandchildren included W.P. Massey, Freelin Dickey, Doll Dickey, Ophelia Dickey, Sally Young, John Robert "Johnny" McIntyre, Adrian McIntyre and Zelphia Whitt.

As early as 1840, Robert was identified as a manufacturer and tradesman, namely a grist miller. He established and operated the first grist mill on Elisha's Branch, which breaks off from Huggins' Creek in the area that is now Finger. Robert's own operation was actually in all probability located in more than one location over the years.

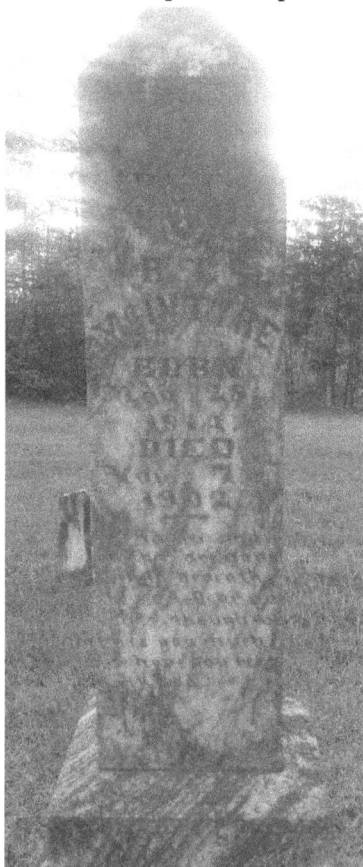

Tombstone of
Robert Thompson McIntyre

Sometime in 1854, Robert bought forty acres from the mulatto Ichabod Brown and located his mill there. The water powered mill was now located on the east side of the creek. However, in less than a year, Robert resold the property to Brown. According to the deed dated April 21, 1855, Robert sold Brown land "containing by estimation forty acres more or less, being the same tract of land you conveyed to me on the 8th of June 1854 and upon which I have Grist Mill now in operation together with the Mill Rocks and all other mill apparatus now in use on said premises." Apparently Robert bought the mill again later, for he was said to have been in the milling business in the latter portion of the nineteenth century.

When there was no milling to do, Robert fished off the back of the porch of the mill building. However, when a customer came by to have their corn ground, they rang a bell so Robert could put his fishing aside and tend to business. After the milling was done and the visiting complete, Robert would go back to his fishing.[58] Besides the milling business, Robert speculated in land and farmed, finding success in both enterprises.

With the formation of the new Republican party in 1854, Robert found a political party to which he and most of his descendents would be loyal for generations to come. In 1858, Robert was elected to the McNairy County Quarterly Court to represent part of north McNairy County. Robert took a strong stance in favor of the Union and its preservation. Therefore he opposed any efforts at secession. McIntyre had an opportunity to be involved in the post-war government that occupied the county seat in Purdy, Tennessee. As it happened, there was no effective operating county government in McNairy County between 1863 and May of 1865. In July of 1865, the new carpet bagger governor of Tennessee, William G. "Parson" Brownlow, appointed various north McNairy countians who had been ardent supporters of the Union to positions of responsibility. McIntyre became Chief Presiding Justice over the McNairy County Quarterly Court and Jacob Lowrance became County Trustee. Within months, McIntyre became Associate Presiding Justice of the Court and remained on the Court until the 1880s.

Robert's wife, Sarah Jane, died on January 12, 1875. He remained active yet unmarried until his remarriage to the widow Ellen Hubanks on November 19, 1876. Whether Ellen died or the marriage was unsuccessful is not known. Apparently the marriage was over by the end of the nineteenth century. It is believed she died and is buried next to Robert in Mount Carmel Cemetery. In his last years, Robert spent time visiting with his grandchildren. Robert was a member of the Church of Christ

---

58. These stories were passed to Robert Thompson McIntyre's grandchildren by him and to other descendants by those grandchildren.

and a member of the International Order of Odd Fellows. He died on November 7, 1902.

Mary Roberta McIntyre (1860–1907)
Farmer and Landowner

Mary Roberta (Coleman) McIntyre is sketched on these pages for the purposes of giving the reader an example of the determination which flowed through the veins of women as well as men. Society has a habit of stereotyping the "settler" as usually a man. Yet there were countless women of strength and courage who helped mold our county and it sons and daughters. One of those was a lady often referred to as "Robertie."

Mary Roberta "Robertie" McIntyre

She was born on February 28, 1860, to John and Isabela Jane Coleman. Her birth was attended to by a mid-wife, Ms. Nancy Maness.[59] Just a few weeks shy of Robertie's third birthday, her father enlisted in the United States Sixth Tennessee Cavalry. Most likely she never remembered much regarding her father, as he died in the summer of 1864 in service to the cause of the Union. Her mother was left to raise her and at least one sister three years her senior. Her marriage to John Absalom McIntyre and their family is mentioned immediately above, therefore no further such factual information is required. Their life, personally and financially, was a good one. By 1896, sixteen years after their marriage, John was the owner of a general store in Finger, a

59. *Affidavit of Nancy Maness* dated March 18, 1871.

substantial farmer and a large-scale land-owner. He owned farms on the edge of present-day Finger stretching from the Mobile and Ohio Railroad to Mount Carmel Cemetery and a large farm at Mount Peter. However, John's untimely and premature death from cancer in 1897 forced Robertie into a role not often assumed by women in that time, that of breadwinner and head of the family.

From 1897 until her death in 1907, Robertie carried on as few women did, given her circumstances and responsibilities. She did not take to the rocking chair and she did not sell off family lands in order to make her way. Instead, she continued farming her husband's grounds and apparently cleared new grounds with the help of two brothers who often worked for her, Lark and Steve Burkeens. Two of the old fields located on her farm were referred to for generations afterwards as the "Lark newground" and the "Steve newground." Old business records from the first decade of the 1900s contain mentions of Robertie's hands and old-

Tombstone of
Mary Roberta (Coleman)
McIntyre

est son, Adrian, bringing loads of crossties to town to sell and there are cotton transactions between Robertie and whoever controlled the gin at any given time. Certainly, Robertie did not resign herself to the role of a passive and inactive widow. Her son, John Robert McIntyre, said often that she was the best farm manager he had ever seen.

Sometime between 1900 and 1907, Robertie moved her family to the village of Finger so that her children would be closer to a school. Her children attended the Possum Trot Schoolhouse, also known as Naylor's Schoolhouse. The family moved into a home which still stands today, the current J.L. Joyner house. It was here the family lived as Robertie continued to own and operate the old farm east of town where her husband lived, worked, and died.

In the winter of 1907, an outbreak of typhoid fever struck the area, carrying away lives and hopes and plans for the future. In this house, an entire family was stricken by this ravenous fever and its winds blew strong against them, eventually carrying away three of the family's beloved members. Radie Sanders, the husband of Zelphia McIntyre and son-in-law of Robertie, became ill and his family cared for him because the McIntyres had enough illness to tend. Radie died shortly thereafter. Robertie herself became too sick to continue and passed away on November 8, 1907. Her oldest daughter, Zenar, followed her home on December 6, 1907. According to family history, Zenar was engaged to Bedford Cone, who was apparently away at the time, and when the letter reached him regarding Zenar's death, his tears smeared the ink on the unfortunate letter. Robertie had seen and suffered much. Yet despite the sorrows of this life, losing her father in the War Between the States, and losing her husband in the full flush of life and success, she carried on. She was buried with her family and her husband in Mount Carmel Cemetery.

William Washington Peeples (1850–1904)
McNairy County Magistrate and Farmer

Squire William Washington "Wash" Peeples was born on November 29, 1850, in Savannah, Hardin County, Tennessee, the son of Henry Calvin Peeples and Susan Elizabeth "Cynthieana" (Malugen) Peeples. The elder Peeples was a law officer in Savannah. During his early years, Wash lived in Kentucky with some of his relatives, the Blakelys.[60] Following Henry Calvin's death sometime around 1858, Susan married William Martin Major Hendrix (1820–1879). Susan died in Columbus, Hickman County, Kentucky, around 1861.

At some point, while he was a young adult, Wash left and went to Arkansas for a while, but upon his return he promised his sweetheart, Bettie Hodges, that he would never leave her again, meaning he would not cross the Mississippi River again. Wash married Elizabeth Ellen

60. For further reference, see the Cotton Ridge article in Chapter Ten of *Let's Call It Finger: A History of North McNairy County and Finger, Tennessee and Its Surrounding Communities* by John E. Talbott, J.D.

William Washington Peebles and his tombstone

"Bettie" Hodges, the daughter of Captain Elijah James Hodges, on November 26, 1882, with William Barney Malone officiating and William Putman acting as bondsman. Wash was a farmer and member of the McNairy County Quarterly Court, and was one of nine members of the Court who voted against removal of the McNairy County seat from Purdy. Little is known about Wash directly. He, his wife, and their son, Eddy, lived near Finger. They resided in close proximity to the Hodges' farm. Bettie "was a very interesting character and a great student, reading much of her time, history being the subject that she liked above others."[61] Wash Peeples died on February 16, 1904, and was buried in the Mount Carmel Cemetery. Bettie Peeples was indeed a well-read and well-educated lady. As stated earlier, she was especially well-versed in history, much like her brothers, Horry and Henry. Bettie passed away on July 29, 1939, and was buried next to her husband.

61. *McNairy County Independent Appeal*, August 4, 1939.

Matthew Ward
First Settler of Mount Carmel Hill

Matthew and Esther Ward migrated to north McNairy County around 1825 and settled on Mount Carmel Hill. He and his wife Esther Ward pitched a tent and moved into it and began the work of establishing a settlement on the old hill. The Wards set out orchards and began turning the wilderness into a settlement. Soon after settling the area, the Wards built a one-room log cabin northwest of Mount Carmel Hill. From Matthew and Esther Ward came good children and respectable citizens. Their children included Luke Ward, Duprina Ward, Lavina (Ward) Weaver, and Nathan Gilbert Ward. Although there is no monument erected to their memory or their graves, it is widely believed that both Matthew and Esther Ward are buried in Mount Carmel Cemetery. Many of their descendants are buried there and the family feels that the first Wards in McNairy County are buried there as well.

Thomas J. Womble (1858–1939)
Farmer and Merchant

Thomas J. "Tom" Womble was born on December 11, 1858, in north McNairy County, Tennessee. He was the son of Manley Womble and wife Mary A. Highfield Womble. His brothers were William A. Womble and Isham Womble. His half-brother was Lee Andrew Weaver, a local banker and businessman. Tom married Louiza "Lucy" E. Walker on January 17, 1884, with Captain Elijah J. Hodges officiating and N.G. Ward standing as bondsman. Lucy was born on October 10, 1860, the daughter of William C. Walker and wife Susan Walker. Tom and Lucy had two daughters, Lula (Womble) McIntyre and Sudie (Womble) Brown. Lula married Sam McIntyre and Sudie married Ily Brown. Tom was a merchant and active in civic affairs in and around Finger, Tennessee. He built the white frame house just past the Mount Carmel Road on present-day Highway 199. According to contemporary sources, Tom inspected every piece of lumber that went into the home. He supposedly rejected every piece of lumber that had a bow or a knot in it.

Tom was an astute businessman. He went into the general merchandise business sometime in the late 1890s. His business records were detailed and he kept careful books. He wisely invested in many of the new banks that sprang up in Mc-Nairy County after the turn of the twentieth century. Tom invested early in Home Banking Company and Selmer Bank and Trust. It was commonly told that he walked down the Mobile and Ohio Railroad tracks to Henderson from Finger with $60,000 on his back.

Thomas J. Womble

Tom was also known for his active lifestyle and stamina. The late Hayes Scott of Tupelo, Mississippi was a grandson of Captain Elijah J. Hodges. He often came to Finger to visit with his aunt Maggie Hodges and uncles Horry, Harmon, and Henry. He also saw Tom on these visits. According to Hayes, he and his uncle Harmon were hunting in the bottoms near the Hodges and Womble homes and the two came across Tom in the woods cutting crossties. At the time, Tom was in his late seventies. Tom died on September 3, 1939, and was buried in the Mount Carmel Cemetery with Rowsey and Morgan Funeral Home in charge. Lucy had preceeded him on March 25, 1926, and was buried in Mount Carmel Cemetery near her parents.

Allen Louis Beene (1826–1890) & Mary Jane Beene (1833–1909)

Allen Louis Beene was the son of William Beene and wife Margaret (Been) Beene and born in Marion County, Tennessee on September 11, 1826.[62] He married Mary Jane Gordon in Tishomingo, Mississippi on November 12, 1848.[63] She was born in South Carolina. The couple had seven children: William Moses Beene, Margaret Rebecca (Beene) McIntyre, Henrietta Beene, John Samuel Beene, Levi Benton Beene,

62. Betty Sitton Reed. *My Three Sons, Volume III: Beene-McIntyre and Allied Lines*. Memphis, TN: Privately published, 1985, page 59. According to the late Mrs. Reed, Margaret Beene's maiden name was Been.

63. *Id*, page 63a

Mary Jane (Gordon) Beene (second from left) with her son John Samuel Beene's family

Martha Ann (Beene) Cobb Schrink, and Malinda Jane (Beene) Walker.[64] Mr. Beene was a farmer. He died on June 24, 1890. Mary Jane Beene lived on and stayed intermittently with her children and their families. Two different family photographs show Mary Jane. In one she is sitting on the porch of the James R. and Margaret Rebecca McIntyre porch and the other sitting with her the family of her son, John Samuel Beene. She died on March 2, 1909, and was buried next to her husband.

Henrietta L. Beene (1874–1899) & Charlie R. Beene (1897–1900)

Henrietta L. Beene was the youngest child of Allen Louis and Mary Jane (Gordon) Beene. She was born on April 3, 1874. According to family sources, Henrietta was mentally challenged and suffered from a form of mental retardation.[65] As oral history has it, Henrietta was walking to a relative's home for a visit when she was set upon by a gang of young men and raped.[66] It resulted in her pregnancy, and she gave birth to a little boy, Charlie R. Beene, on April 1, 1897. Although it is not known with

64. *Id*, page 60

65. *Id*, and interview with Robert Beene, the son of John Samuel Beene.

66. *Id*.

The tombstones of Henrietta L. Beene (left) and her son Charlie R. Beene

certainty, Henrietta and the child likely remained with her mother. In keeping with her already tragic life, Henrietta became ill and died at the age of age of 25 on October 2, 1899. Young Charlie was not destined to live long either. He died on April 4, 1900 at the tender young age of three.

Malissa America (Coleman) Beene (1857–1919)

Malissa America (Coleman) Beene was born on June 7, 1857, the daughter of John Coleman and wife Isabella Jane (Causey) Coleman. At the time of her birth, her mother was attended to by Elizabeth Murry (Murray), a midwife.[67] In January 1863, when Malissa was only five and her sister, Mary Roberta Coleman (later McIntyre) was only two, their

67. Affidavit of Elizabeth Murry dated March 13, 1871, as witnessed by R.M. Thompson and Eli Thomas before Calvin Shull, Clerk of the McNairy County Court, and Affidavit of Elizabeth of Murry under examination dated June 18, 1872 before Justice of the Peace Robert D. Wilson in the presence of witnesses J.M. Harris and R.B. Turner. These affidavit and examinations were conducted for the purpose of proving relations for the pension of Isabella Jane Coleman regarding the death of her husband John Coleman during the American Civil War in which he served as a Private in the Company A of the U.S. Sixth Tennessee Cavalry.

father, John Coleman, cast his lot with the Union cause and enlisted in the U.S. Sixth Tennessee Cavalry in Bolivar, Tennessee. He served in Company A of this unit and fought under the command of Colonel Fielding Hurst. His service to the Union cause ended on June 28, 1864, when he died in Memphis, Tennessee of chronic diarrhea (most likely some form of dysentery).[68] He was buried in the National Cemetery within feet of his fellow soldiers and neighbors, Isaac McIntyre and Captain Horry Hodges, all of whom died in 1864.

At the time, many Unionist familieswere forced to emigrate to the southern regions of Northern states. Many West Tennesseans made their way to southern Illinois. In some cases, the move was made to avoid having a teenage son drafted or conscripted into Confederate service. In other cases, local Unionist families were concerned about retribution for their loyalty to the Union cause. Isabella Jane, Malissa America, and Mary Roberta all settled temporarily in Nashville, Washington County, Illinois sometime during the course of the war. The

Malissa America (Coleman) Beene (right) with unidentified man and her sister Mary Roberta (Coleman) McIntyre

---

68. *Widow's Declaration to the Department at Washington for Army Pension* submitted by Isabella J. Coleman dated June 17, 1865, with the assistance of Amos Watts, Attorney at Law of Nashville, Illinois.

three were definitely living in Illinois as of June 17, 1865, and were still there in the spring of 1866.[69]

Eventually, the trio came home. The exact facts concerning Malissa America's personal life are somewhat in dispute. According to family sources, Malissa married Pleasant Henry and they had children. A photograph was found among the papers of Vivian and Lessie McIntyre, the great-nieces of Malissa America Coleman, of a Pleasant Henry and wife. The wife in the photograph strongly favored images of a younger Malissa America Coleman. However, there is no record for such a union in McNairy County. However, there are records for a marriage between a M.A. Coleman and F.C. Robertson in 1879, and a Malissa Coleman and a Henry Hodge in 1872. The bondman for the Coleman-Hodge union was a J.F. Dillon. One must remember that she was related to the Dillons.

In any event, she married William Moses Beene. Mr. Beene was a widower and had a number of children by his first wife, Amanda (Dickey) Beene. He and Malissa America had at least two children: a daughter named S.C.B. Beene and a son named E.H. Beene. Malissa America was mentioned by John Carlyle Parsons in his memoirs:

> She [Malissa America Coleman] married William Beene, a widower and had several children by him. I visited them in 1910 when they lived at Henderson, Tennessee, a few miles from Finger. Mrs. Beene and I drove in a buggy to Finger to see Jim McIntyre, who was one of my father's boyhood friends and the brother of the man who married Roberta, the other Coleman daughter.[70]

Malissa America (Coleman) Beene died on June 16, 1919.

Francis C. "France" Clayton (1841–1925)

Francis C. "France" Clayton is the lone Confederate grave in the Mount Carmel Cemetery. Frankly, little is known about Clayton. It is believed that he was a brother to Robert M. Clayton. The two are

69. *Claim for Widow's Pension (War of 1861)* dated March 6, 1866 filed by Isabella J. Coleman and Amos Watts, Attorney at Law.

70. John Carlyle Parsons. *History of One Parsons Family*. 1938.

Tombstone of Francis M. Clayton

buried within a few feet of one another and in the 1860 U.S. Census, there is a male identified as Franklin Clayton living with Robert M. Clayton and his wife Mary C. Clayton.[71] The individual whose name was later transcribed as Franklin was born in the same period of time as France Clayton.

It is known that Francis C. "France" Clayton enlisted in the Confederate Thirteenth Tennessee Infantry. According to that regiment's commander, Colonel A.J. Vaughan, in his work, *Personal Record of the Thirteenth Regiment, Tennessee Infantry, C.S.A.*, Francis Clayton was a soldier in Company F and living around Montezuma, Tennessee after the war.[72] In fact, Clayton probably received his mail at the Montezuma Post Office in 1897 when the book was published.

Clayton's unit, Company F, was known as "The Wright Boys." The company was originally commanded by two of Purdy, Tennessee's finest young men, John Vines Wright (also its recent U.S. Congressman) and Dew Moore Wisdom as well as G.W. Churchwell.[73] As far as can be ascertained, France Clayton was engaged in the following battles during the War Between the States: the battle of Belmont, Missouri, the battle of Pittsburg Landing (Shiloh), the battle of Richmond, Kentucky, the battle of Perryville, Kentucky, the battle of Murfreesboro, Tennessee, the battle of Chickamauga, and the retreat from Atlanta, Georgia after its fall. Clayton had the opportunity to travel all over the South during his time in the Thirteenth Infantry. Clayton and his colleagues were in-

71. The 1860 U.S. Census spelled the name Clayton as "Claton."

72. A.J. Vaughan. *Personal Record of the Thirteenth Regiment, Tennessee Infantry, C.S.A.* Memphis, TN: S.C. Toof & Co. Press, 1897. Reprinted by Frank & Gennie Myers and Burke's Book Store, Memphis, Tennessee.

73. *Tennesseans in the Civil War: A Military History of Confederate and Union Units with Available Rosters of Personnel, Part 1.* Nashville, TN: Civil War Centennial Commission, 1964.

volved in a number of actions and activities short of battle and their activities were constant.

Isabel Jane Coleman (1825–1891)

Isabel Jane Causey was born on May 18, 1825. She was first married to a gentleman by the name of Joseph Fremont Parsons in Greensboro, North Carolina.[74] She later married John Coleman on December 26, 1852, with William Lane, a minister, officiating.[75] She and John Coleman had two daughters, Malissa America Coleman and Mary Roberta "Robertie" Coleman. Malissa was born on June 7, 1857, with a midwife, Elizabeth Murry, assisting.[76] On February 28, 1860, Robertie was born. With the outbreak of the War Between the States, the Coleman family, like all families, found their future uncertain. With the Confederate loss at Pittsburg Landing (Shiloh), John Coleman enlisted in the United States Sixth Tennessee Cavalry, a unit commanded by Colonel Fielding Hurst, in LaGrange, Tennessee.

During John's service in the Union Army, Isabel and their daughters fled to Washington County, Illinois. They resided in the

Isabel Jane Coleman

74. Parsons, *History of One Parsons Family.*

75. *Widow's Declaration to the Department at Washington for Army Pension* of Isabel Jane Coleman dated June 17, 1865,

76. *Affidavit of Elizabeth Murry* dated June 18, 1872.

town of Nashville for the duration of the war. It must be kept in mind that many Union sympathizers fled to southern Illinois during the course of the war. It is not known if the Coleman family knew someone in Illinois, but it is probable that they did. Her future son-in-law, John A. McIntyre, a teenager at the time, was also in southern Illinois in the same area. How Isabel was able to sustain herself and her daughters in Illinois is not known. Where they resided or with whom is not known either.

John Coleman was attached to Company A. He was born circa 1819, and served from January 7, 1863 until his death on July 27, 1864. He was hospitalized at Washington Hospital in Memphis, Tennessee and being treated by Assistant Surgeon E.C. Strode, M.D. According to the Surgeon General's Office in a report dated February 27, 1866, John Coleman died of chronic diarrhea. He was buried in the National Cemetery in Memphis, Tennessee within a few feet of his old neighbors, Captain Horry Hodges and Isaac McIntyre, the son of Robert Thompson McIntyre and brother of John A. McIntyre. While still in Illinois, Isabel made the decision to apply for a widow's pension. She employed an attorney by the name of Amos Watts from Nashville, Illinois. With Watt's assistance, she was able to procure a pension to assist her in her efforts to provide for Malissa and Robertie.

Isabel eventually returned to north McNairy County with her daughters. At some point, she lived in a small log cabin just off what is now Centerhill Road across the road from where the sawmill is presently located.[77] After Robertie married John A. McIntyre, Isabel lived with John and Robertie. However, according to oral history handed down by her grandson, John Robert McIntyre, Isabel became angry with her son-in-law, John, when he would not carry Isabel to Purdy to retrieve her pension check from the post office. She wanted to go to Purdy on the day that it would have normally arrived, but John was busy and could not go for a few days. This angered Isabel and she moved out of their house. She died on August 20, 1891.

77. The site is now owned and utilized by Danny Beachy as a shop and equipment yard.

Maggie Hodges (1876–1955)
Educator and Socialite

Maggie Hodges, the youngest daughter of Elijah J. Hodges and wife Nancy Jane (Dodd) Hodges, was born on March 27, 1876, in the vicinity of what would later be known as Finger, Tennessee. She lived her entire life in the home that served as the family seat for generations. She was a beautiful young woman and very refined. Like her brothers and sisters she was well-educated and well-read, and her talents and intellect were recognized by others. She began her life as an educator.

Maggie was the only one of the Hodges' daughters who did not marry. She was close to her brothers Horry, Henry, Harmon, and Harvey. At the time of their father's death in 1913, it is believed that the five remaining unmarried children—Maggie, Horry, Henry, Harmon, and Harvey—signed a pact pledging to never marry and to remain at the family home to care for their elderly mother and to preserve the family home.

Despite her affection for her older brothers, Maggie was especially close to her younger brother, Harvey, who was two years younger than her. These two siblings were close in age and spent much time together growing up. According to some sources Harvey was afflicted with tuberculosis, and tradition says that Maggie kept careful watch over him during periods of sickness.

Maggie Hodges

There was much discussion regarding Harvey's engagement to Miss Ethel Plunk, the daughter of C.C. Plunk and a colleague of Harvey's in the education field. It has been alleged that Maggie was vociferous in her objection to Harvey's engagement to Miss Plunk. According to family sources and those familiar with the circumstances, Maggie objected on political and personal grounds and because Harvey was reneging on his pledge to remain unmarried and assist in taking care of the family estate. Interestingly, Harvey's decision to marry Miss Plunk came less than a year after Nancy Jane (Dodd) Hodges' death.

Maggie remained unmarried herself. Although she had taught at Lain's Academy in her early years, she did not work outside the home for decades. Instead she acted as hostess of the Hodges' family and Hodges' home and was known as a dignified and congenial hostess. Many individuals recalled in later life the gracefulness of Maggie Hodges and her wit and intellect. Often she and her brothers had neighbors in their home on holidays and for special events. Neighbor Faye (McIntyre) Talbott recalled visiting Maggie with her mother, Ollie Pearl McIntyre, and sitting out in the yard beneath large oak trees while the ladies talked and visited. In her later years, Sue (Hampton) Robison recalled spending Christmas Eve with the Hodges in 1930. Folks recalled her pretty lamps, her intelligent banter, and her interesting but liberated style of dress. Maggie often visited friends in Selmer and was a welcomed visitor to many old acquaintances. The late Guy Brown once recalled carrying Maggie, Horry, Henry, and Harmon to pick up a new automobile. Brown recalled listening in on the foursome's conversation. According to Brown, the four talked incessantly during the entire trip to Selmer and found their conversation thoroughly entertaining and informative.

Maggie and Harmon lost their brothers, Horry and Henry, in 1940 and 1941 respectively. The two continued to stay at the old home place until October 30, 1955, when Maggie passed away at the age of 79. She was buried nearby the rest of the family, and Harmon would be buried next to her a couple of years later in 1957.

Allen R. Womble (1885–1909)
Memphis Streetcar Conductor

Allen R. Womble was born on July 4, 1885, the son of William B. Womble and wife Mary E. (Beene) Womble. Surviving photographs show that he was a handsome young man. He married Miss Bettie Naylor on July 23, 1905, with Horry Hodges acting as his bondman and Justice of the Peace of C.C. Plunk officiating. It appears that they had at least two children, Carl Womble and Mary Womble. Mary died in 1910 at

Allen R. Womble worked as a street-car conductor (left and below) in Memphis, Tennessee in the early 1900s. He was killed while driving his streetcar in 1909. He had just turned 24 years old.

less than one year of age. At some point after 1905, Allen and his wife moved to Memphis, Tennessee, where Allen worked as a streetcar conductor. He conducted Streetcar No. 533, and it was in this profession that Allen would lose his life while still a very young man. According to a newspaper at the time, Allen became a "first class conductor." On Friday, July 30, 1909, the car he was driving was struck by a switch engine as it crossed the railroad tracks. Allen was killed instantly and a number of his passengers were seriously hurt. His body was sent to Finger and he was buried in Mount Carmel Cemetery.

Alfred Monroe Plunk (1836–1918)
Farmer and Soldier

Alfred Monroe Plunk was born in 1836 to George Plunk and wife Fanny (Jarman) Plunk. Like many young men in north McNairy County, Tennessee, Alfred Monroe Plunk was swept up in the War Between the States. His account and that of his brother was previously published in *Let's Call It Finger! A History of North McNairy County and Finger, Tennessee and Its Surrounding Communities,* and is as follows:

> According to family tradition, brothers Alfred Monroe Plunk and Daniel David Plunk went to the county seat, Purdy, and were more or less coerced into joining the Confederate Army. Concerned about their plight, the two brothers went to seek advice from an elderly gentleman by the name of Lane. Mister Lane told them, "Boys, join and then desert." Therefore, in September of 1861, the two joined the Confederate Army. However, they were put off a train at Henderson Station in February of 1862 as both of them were suffering from smallpox. Daniel passed away and Alfred's clothes were laid out for his burial, but surprisingly he survived. In July of 1862, Alfred was declared a deserter.
>
> The Confederates came looking for Alfred at his parents' place on Tar Creek on at least two occasions. On one occasion, Alfred ran toward the woods "with Confederate bullets kicking up the dirt behind him and all around him." On another occasion, the local Confederate authorities came riding

up to the Plunk homestead and the commander of the group called out, "Strike a light!" This meant "who's in the house?" Alfred was hiding out in the loft of the house and sleeping on cottonseed which was stored there. The family could distinctly hear Alfred moving around in the loft to a suitable hiding place. Alfred quickly made his way to the dark corner where the chimney stood and there he hid. A Confederate stuck his head up in the loft and looked around before calling to the others, "Nobody here."

It was during these times that many in north McNairy County, a hotbed of Union loyalty and activity, tired of any Confederate presence. There was occasional harassment by Confederates of the Unionist populace in north McNairy County and according to one source, there was some conflict along Tar Creek. According to this story, the local Unionists in desperation decided to lay an ambush for the marauding and harassing Rebels. About a dozen Unionists were lying low along the run of Tar Creek when they waylaid the unsuspecting Rebels, injuring at least one. Another Confederate had his horse shot out from under him and as he chased after the others on foot, the amused and satisfied Unionists laughingly called out, "Look at him run! Look at him run!" Alfred Monroe Plunk was present for this event and followed after the now-afoot Rebel with the others and eventually captured him. Needing a wagon to transport the wounded man, they sought and received help from Calloway Robison, a local blacksmith.[78]

Alfred Monroe Plunk was married twice and had numerous children. He married first to Emily Caroline Dickey, the daughter of John A. Dickey and wife Sarah Dickey. She was a sister of George Dickey, who married Amanda McIntyre. Alfred and Emily married on November 25, 1869, with the Reverend Wilson A. McHolstead officiating. The couple had five children: Elijah Lawson Plunk, Robert Levi Plunk, Jacob Andrew Plunk, Susan A. Plunk, and Sarah Frances Plunk. Emily

78. John E. Talbott, J.D. *Let's Call It Finger! A History of North McNairy County and Finger, Tennessee and Its Surrounding Communities*. Henderson, TN: Privately published, 2003.

Tombstones of Alfred Monroe Plunk

Caroline Plunk died in 1879 and was buried in Mount Carmel Cemetery. In December of 1879, Alfred Monroe Plunk married Catherine M. "Kizzie" Dunn, the daughter of John Dunn. They had ten children: Amanda Ann Plunk, Chester Arthur Plunk, Nancy Ellen Plunk, Albert James Plunk, Daisy Florence Plunk, Ollie Catherine Plunk, John Clay Plunk, Jessie Millard Plunk, Minnie Irene Plunk, and Lucy Edna Plunk. According to the late Rachel Hooper, a granddaughter of Elisha Lawson Plunk, Catherine M. "Kizzie" Dunn Plunk had a daughter by the name of Violet at the time she married Alfred Monroe Plunk. In 1918, Alfred Monroe Plunk died and "Kizzie" followed him in death in 1925.

Arthur Marion Douglas "Whig" McCann (1859–1937)
Farmer

Arthur Marion Douglas "Whig" McCann was born in McNairy County on April 11, 1859, the eldest son of Doctor W. "Dock" McCann and wife Eliza Ann (Rose) McCann. He was married on April 22, 1879, to Parthenia A. Tacker, the daughter of Thomas M. Tacker and wife Narcissa (Barnes) Tacker. Whig and Parthenia had nine children: Truman Pleasant McCann, Arthur Columbus "Arter" McCann, William Andrew "Ander" McCann, Lillie Ophelia (McCann) Ward, Noah Ernest McCann, Ollie Pearl (McCann) McIntyre, Parthenia A. McCann, Victoria

A. McCann, and Harriet Lutisha (McCann) Rouse. The McCann children attended Lain's Academy. They recalled in their old age with great warmth their father's musical abilities. Whig was especially talented on the fiddle. His children and grandchildren readily recalled him playing such playful tunes as "Pop Goes the Weasel" while sitting by the hearth on cold winter evenings while a fire burned in the fireplace. Other songs which he played for all of his children included "8th of January," "Sheepshead and a Thousand Dumplins," and "Dog Tree'd a 'Possum."[79]

The children of Whig and Parthenia were also very talented. Most of them played some form of musical instrument. Their daughter, Ollie Pearl, could play the guitar, mandolin, and the juice harp. She and her brothers regularly serenaded young newly mar-

Arthur Marion Douglas "Whig" McCann

ried couples and others on their birthday. Music was an important part of their family. These children readily recalled a father who was warm and kind and a genuine family man.

Whig was a talented and industrious farmer and appears to have enjoyed life. However, there also was sadness in his life. Sometime in 1906, Parthenia became ill. Eventually, it would be learned that she was suffering from breast cancer. She was presented with the option of having an operation to remove the cancer, most likely a mastectomy. However, she was fearful of the operation for she greatly feared pain. Like many women of her day, she was at once fragile and rugged. She continued to be active until nearly the end. She sewed and knitted for friends and neighbors. The cancer progressed so aggressively that eventually her beating heart

79. Kevin D. McCann. *The McCanns of McNairy County, Tennessee: A History of the Descendants of John McCann Senior.* Ashland City, TN: Privately published, 1995.

could be seen through a sore in her chest. Her daughter, Ollie Pearl, was charged with the responsibility of changing her bandages as her daughter, Lillie, did not have the constitution or stomach to perform the task.

Whig and Parthenia lived in a two-story log cabin with a dogtrot on the farm now known as the Bill Cone farm. The house was located on a small knob just off the present-day Payne Road. It was here that Parthenia McCann died on March 7, 1907. She was laid to rest in the Chapel Hill Cemetery near her infant daughters, Parthenia and Victoria, and her mother, Narcissa Barnes Tacker.

Within a few months of Parthenia's death, Whig would remarry. He married Cordelia H. "Celia" Weaver, the daughter of his friends Absalom Weaver, Jr. and Tilda Emaline Henson Weaver, on July 2, 1907. Whig was forty-eight years old at the time and Celia was fourteen. Between 1910 and 1931, the couple had twelve children. Those children were: Mamie McCann, A.D. McCann, Wilmer McCann, Ola McCann, Jim Dell McCann, Jessie Nola (McCann) Davis, Arthur Marion "Pat" McCann, Beulah Mae (McCann) Vance Van Wart, Nancy Virginia (McCann) Cogdell, Georgia Allen (McCann) Huey, Hazel McCann, and Ava Lee (McCann) Kaufman.

Whig was a Methodist by belief. He enjoyed fatherhood and continued farming, raising children, playing music and making sorghum molasses into his seventies. His life was good and he took time to visit with his grown children and his grandchildren. In 1935, he discovered that he had cancer on his lower lip. He traveled to Memphis for experimental radium treatments, but there was little that could be done to prevent its spread. To keep him cool and to prevent wearing out the individuals fanning him, his son-in-law, John Robert McIntyre, designed and built a fan that could be easily pulled by a chain. The fan kept Whig cool on hot days and nights during the period when he was bedfast. Whig McCann died on August 24, 1937, and was buried in Mount Carmel Cemetery.

Truman Pleasant McCann (1880–1948)
Farmer and Photographer

Truman Pleasant McCann was born in McNairy County, Tennessee, on December 30, 1880, to Arthur Marion Douglas "Whig" McCann and wife Parthenia A. Tacker McCann. He attended school at Lain's Academy and farmed in his early life. As a young man, he endured a life-changing event. While plowing a new ground, his plow struck a root which in turn struck his leg and caused an injury. In time, the leg became infected and had to be amputated. The limb was placed in a wooden box and buried in Mount Carmel Cemetery.

The loss of his right leg forced Truman to seek out other professions. At times, he worked as a retail salesman and ran a hamburger stand. He became very interested in the photography business. He experimented with the various aspects of the profession and built a darkroom onto his house. In 1908, the Mc-Nairy County Quarterly Court

Truman Pleasant McCann

granted Truman a license to "make pictures" in McNairy County, thus beginning a new career. That year, he married Ila Elizabeth "Ily" Womble on February 17, 1908, with Justice of the Peace J.E. Barham officiating. The couple had five children: Mary A. McCann, Fred McCann, Albert McCann, Jewell (McCann) Maxwell, and R.B. McCann. The couple later divorced in Alcorn County, Mississippi on March 20, 1928.

In the north McNairy County area during the period of the 1910s through the 1930s, Truman McCann photographed countless individuals and families. He developed the plates in his homemade darkroom. One of his nieces well recalled decades later having gotten into his darkroom and Truman coming in and running her and her cousins out of it.

One interesting story regarding Truman involved his amputated leg. Sometime after it was taken off, he began to feel a biting and cramped sensation from his amputated leg! He talked his brothers into going up to Mount Carmel Cemetery, digging up the leg, and placing it in a bigger box. His brothers, apparently very faithful, did as he requested. After placing it inside a larger box, Truman never had any further sensations from the troublesome limb.

Truman had a good sense of humor and was close to his siblings. His nieces and nephews were often spooked by his false leg. He would take the leg off and prop it against the wall or by the door, and he laughed as his nieces and nephews would hide from him. After he and Ily divorced, Truman married a second time to Fannie Victoria (Calburn) McGaugh in Alcorn County, Mississippi on April 22, 1933. That marriage too ended in divorce. Truman later developed tuberculosis and his first wife Ily took care of him at her home in Corinth, Mississippi. He lingered in an unhealthy state until his death there on March 5, 1948.

John Robert McIntyre (1893–1989)
Farmer, Machinist, and Broom Maker

John Robert McIntyre's early life was reminiscent of a tale by Charles Dickens. A young man born into great prospect and respectability with great opportunities before him, he was orphaned at any early age and forced to face great strife and a life of hard work and struggle. He was born on July 27, 1893, the middle son of John Absalom McIntyre and Mary Roberta (Coleman) McIntyre. At the time of his birth, his father was steadily building a bright and prosperous future for his family. Unfortunately, his father fell ill with skin cancer in 1897 and died leaving his wife and young children. His widow purchased a home in Finger in order to have her children closer to a school, in this case, the Possum Trot Schoolhouse or Naylor's Schoolhouse. John Robert, along with his mother and siblings, lived in the home that would later become the J.L. Joyner home. They also spent considerable time out at the McIntyre farm.

In 1907, when he was fourteen, John and his entire family fell ill with typhoid fever. By the time the fever had swept through the family, it had carried off in death his mother Mary Roberta McIntyre, his sister Zenar McIntyre, and his brother-in-law Radie Sanders. Radie's family came and retrieved him and he died while in their care. Mary Roberta died on November 8, 1907, at her Finger home, which was later known as the Clayton home and the J.L. Joyner home. On the day of his mother's funeral, John Robert McIntyre was wrapped in a blanket and sitting next to his mother's grave during the funeral services. He was fourteen and alone.

His future wife, thirteen year old Ollie Pearl McCann, was present and never forgot the sight of the sad young man staring out from the blanket at his mother's casket. After Mary Roberta's death, John was left in a home still in the shadow of death.

On December 6, 1907, John Robert's sister Zenar died of typhoid fever. One photograph of Zenar survives which shows a beautiful young woman with every appearance of a bright demeanor. In fact, John Robert never forgot his sister. He once very lovingly and deliberately pointed out her grave to the author and attempted to describe her, but became emotional and moved on

John Robert McIntyre

to point out his parents' graves. Family tradition holds that Zenar was engaged to Bedford Cone and that he learned of her death after receiving a letter to that effect. According to the family tale, his tears stained the ink on the letter as he read of her death.

With the death of three immediate family members, John Robert's family moved on. With no one upon whom to depend, John had to plan to live independently at age fourteen. He and his sister Zelphia Sanders, now a widow, determined to make a crop together. They set about putting in a crop in the spring of 1908 and made it through the winter. They set about again to survive 1909 in the same manner.

However, just as the two were planning to put in another crop, Zelphia married William Harrison Whitt on March 3, 1909, with Ed Barham officiating. There were few people whom John Robert genuinely detested, but Whitt was among that few. Whitt was a rowdy man with a mean spirit. Young John Robert had an early aversion to strong drink as his father was an active Freemason, member of the Church of Christ, and believer in temperance. One day, Whitt physically overwhelmed the young man and forced him to swallow some whiskey. It was the only alcohol that he ever drank, and he never forgave Whitt for forcing it upon him.[80]

Sometime in 1910, John Robert went to Corinth and worked for a foundry as a machinist. This foundry provided parts and materials for the locks and mechanisms used in the Panama Canal. While living in Corinth, he learned a considerable amount about the work of a machinist and gained a love for tinkering and invention. He realized that he had a knack for such talents. He also realized that he was in love with young Ollie Pearl McCann. During this period while residing in Corinth, he began to write regular letters to her in Finger. She kept these letters until her death in 1980. The author recalls standing next to his great-grand-father, John Robert, while he showed the letters to visitors at her wake. The author still recalls a tearful old man holding the letters tied in a ribbon. He would pull them out of his suit coat and show them to a visitor and place them carefully back in his coat pocket. In fact, he buried the letters with her on that February day in 1980.

In an interview conducted by Marvin Hand of Hesperia, California, on March 2, 1982, John Robert recounted his marriage and life with Ollie Pearl McCann. He stated:

> On Saturday, August 12, 1911, I married Ollie Pearl Mc-
> Cann. We were married by Justice of the Peace Isom Naylor
> over in the edge of Chester County. We were married sitting

80. Zelphia would later be left a widow again when Whitt's mean streak manifested itself. According to an account previously published in *Let's Call it Finger! A History of North McNairy County and Finger, Tennessee and Its Surrounding Communities*:

"William Whitt's death could have been prevented, but in his haste to kill Grover McDaniel, he accidentally put the nails in his own coffin. For whatever reason, on late Friday afternoon, June 11, 1926, Whitt and McDaniel, while in the course of arguing got rough and tumble. Whitt, a man of some height and size, grabbed McDaniel, a much smaller and shorter individual, and held McDaniel against himself with McDaniel's back pressed against his own chest and then shot McDaniel. According to one source, Whitt pointed the muzzle of the pistol at the top of McDaniel's head and the bullet traveled through McDaniel's body downwards before striking Whitt in the chest. The 1926 newspaper report on the shooting stated that McDaniel died instantly and that 'Whitt received a wound in the abdomen, and was hurried to a hospital in Corinth.' The report went on to say that a warrant charging Whitt with first degree murder was sworn out." Whitt would die on June 18, 1926, and would be buried at Mount Carmel. He lay in an unmarked grave until approximately 1999 when his granddaughter, Tanya Becker, erected a monument to his memory and his grave as well as that of his father.

John Robert McIntye and his wife Ollie Pearl (McCann) McIntyre were known for their handmade brooms

in the buggy at Squire Naylor's home, which is now the Glenn Naylor place.

We had planned on being married on Sunday, but when we heard that a crowd planned on being there for the wedding, we decided to get married on Saturday instead, as we were quite bashful. We had six children: Helen, who is deceased, Lessie, Roy, Vivian, Faye and J.R.

My wife, Ollie Pearl, was born October 7, 1894. From our marriage in 1911 until her death in 1980, we had 69 happy years together. We worked hard and had some tough times during which we raised six children.

I have sold corn for fifty cents a bushel and have sawed firewood and hauled it to Finger, cut to length and ready to burn, for $4.00 a cord.

We had some wet years and some dry years which hurt all of the farmers. A dry year was 1913 when I made only 2 bales of cotton on 8 acres. The year 1927 was so wet we could hardly see the young cotton stalks for the grass.

We had a tough time thinning the cotton and cutting the grass from around the young cotton and corn.[81]

One of John Robert's well-known traits was his knack for invention and tinkering in order to save labor and make it more efficient and effective. When he inherited his portion of his father's farm, his roughly 100 acre portion included a wet bottomland slough than ran through the heart of it. John Robert determined to drain this land and make it productive. Therefore, he determined to build his own homemade ditcher or backhoe. He used a kerosene engine to power it and built an apparatus that supported a dirt bucket operated by ropes, chains, and pulleys. He fashioned a piece of sheet metal into a bucket and attached cultivator teeth on it. It held a little more than a five gallon bucket of soil. He rolled the contraption down into the bottom on logs and began to cutting a new course for Bushel Creek. Today, the new run is located along John Robert's path. The contraption attracted attention and people came down to see it operate. He often tinkered with hand tools and converted them into motorized tools. When his father-in-law, Whig McCann, became ill and his caregivers grew physically tired while fanning him to keep him cool, John Robert devised a fan that could be operated using a foot pedal and chain whereby one person could fan Whig all day without growing tired.

In his early life with a growing family, he began to look for other avenues for income. He discovered broom making after visiting with a Mr. Phillips in the neighborhood and observed his operation. He returned home and began building his own equipment and entered into a vocation which would occupy him for decades. In the fall of 2012, John Robert and Ollie Pearl McIntyre were honored by the Tennessee Folklore Society in an epitaph written for the *Tennessee Folklore Society Bulletin* by Dr. Shawn Pitts regarding the proud broomcorn and broom making tradition of McNairy County.[82] John survived Ollie Pearl by almost a decade before dying on September 19, 1989, at the age of 96.

81. Marvin Hand. "Notes Taken While Talking to John Robert McIntyre at Finger, Tennessee, March 2, 1982."

82. Dr. Shawn Pitts. "McNairy County Brooms: Better and Cheaper Than Any Brought On." *Tennessee Folklore Society Bulletin*, Volume LXV, Number 2, Fall 2012, Knoxville, Tennessee. This edition was incorrectly identified as being the Fall 2009 edition.

R. Jenkins Miller (1870–1951)
Hobo and Traveler

R. Jenkins Miller was more commonly known to friends and acquaintances as "Red" Miller. He was the son of Issac Miller and Esbell (Isbell) Fowler Miller. In 1860, Esbell Fowler was 18 years old and living in the household of Jack and Elizabeth Walsh in the Anderson Store community. Isaac Miller's background is currently unknown. However, he married Esbell Fowler on or about August 22, 1870. Their marriage certificate lists their names as Elizabeth Fowler and Isham Miller. Interestingly, Red's date of birth was June 19, 1870. His father was still alive as of 1881. Red was best known as a hobo who rode the rails from Canada to Mexico. His exploits inspired young men who dreamed of adventures across the continent.

Red taught many young men the small things of hobo life: hobo cuisine, how to spot a friendly home where food could be procured and where kindness could be found, and how to survive on the rails. Many thought him to be mentally challenged and indeed he appears to have been quite peculiar. One memory shared by a number of knowledgeable people was that Red would curse a tormentor and then pray that a

Tombstone of R. Jenkins "Red" Miller and his mother,
which was paid for by those who knew him

rock would fall on the offending person's head. He was often teased and perhaps tormented by some.

Red's knowledge of the country's rail system was apparently unquestioned. Again, he was reputed to have traveled the 48 contiguous states, Canada, and Mexico. One story demonstrates his knowledge and resourcefulness on the rails. He was related in some way or another to the Finis E. Miller family of Finger. Apparently, he visited Miller's spinster daughters, Mattie and Callie, only to learn that he had just missed a visit from other members of the family who lived in one of the western states. Thereupon learning that he had indeed missed these relatives and that they had already left the state on their return trip, Red struck out after them. When these western relatives arrived at home, they found Red sitting on their front porch awaiting their arrival. He had beaten them home.

Red continued to live the life of the hobo until such time that he became unable to travel. At some point, he left the Finger area and went to the Poor House at Selmer to live. Members of the community came down to the Finger Depot to see Red Miller off. He lived out the rest of his life there and died on August 16, 1951, of a coronary thrombosis due to hypertensive cardiovascular disease. He was buried at Mount Carmel and local townsfolk raised funds to purchase a gravestone for him and his mother. It is not known currently if his father is buried there as well.

CHAPTER FOUR

✧

MOUNT CARMEL CEMETERY CENSUS

This chapter contains an updated census of the Mount Carmel Cemetery. The list which follows contains the names of some 400 individuals. Several of these graves once occupied the unmarked and unknown column. Thankfully after much research and time, more than thirty graves have been reclaimed. This list will appear alphabetically.

1. Ada, A.L., nephew of J.L. & Susan Hubanks (November 24, 1898–September 3, 1904)
2. Ash, J.W. (September 25, 1833–September 7, 1898)[1]
3. Ash, Mary Virginia (April 19, 1854–May 27, 1941)

---

1. J.W. Ash and wife Sarah M. Ash were the parents of Quincy Ash, the man who famously disappeared in or around the year 1909.

4. Ash, Sarah M. (1835–May 23, 1915)[2]
5. Barker, Ida Elizabeth Floyd (September 14, 1900–October 30, 1918) unmarked grave
6. Barnes, Emily Elizabeth Lain, wife of Henry Calvin Barnes and daughter of James Lain and Cinthia Dennis Lain (January 21, 1832–July 20, 1918) unmarked grave
7. Barnes, Henry Calvin (May 5, 1822- October 20, 1898) unmarked grave
8. Barnes, Henry White, son of H.C. & E.E.L. Barnes; father of Arky and Ida Barnes (born October 22, 1863–?) unmarked grave
9. Barnes, J.A. (April 3, 1858–January 12, 1885)
10. Beecham, Missouri[3] (no dates)
11. Beene, Allen Louis (September 14, 1826–June 24, 1890)
12. Beene, Charlie R., son of Henrietta L. Beene (April 1, 1897–April 4, 1900)
13. Beene, E.H., son of W.A. & M.A. Beene (August 29, 1888–May 13, 1901)
14. Beene, Henrietta L., daughter of A.L. & M.J. Beene (April 3, 1874–October 2, 1899)[4]
15. Beene, Malissa America (Coleman), wife of W.M. Beene (June 7, 1857–June 16, 1919)
16. Beene, Mary Jane, wife of A.L. Beene (December 27, 1833–March 2, 1909)[5]
17. Beene, S.C.B., daughter of W.M. & M.A. Beene (July 27, 1879–August 29, 1897)
18. Beene, William Moses (1849–1927)
19. Boyd, George (1909–2000)
20. Boyd, Jewell Cayce (1918–1999)[6]
21. Boyd, Kenneth Alton (February 28, 1939–April 19, 2009)

2. Sarah M. Ash's maiden name was Floyd. *McNairy County, Tennessee Death Book, 1908-1912.* McNairy County Records Commission.

3. Missouri Beecham was an elderly lady who lived with Dan Griswell's sisters.

4. Sadly, Henrietta Beene was born mentally retarded and never married. According to members of the Beene family, Henrietta was raped by a group of young men while walking from her parents' house to another relative's house. Afterward, she gave birth to Charlie.

5. Mary Jane Beene's maiden name was Fuller.

6. Jewell Boyd's maiden name was Griffin.

22. Boyd, Tommy (no dates)[7]
23. Boyd, William Jerry (October 20, 1937–October 18, 1938)
24. Brown, Buddie (June 22, 1892–October 4, 1899)[8]
25. Brown, Cornelius[9] (no dates)
26. Brown, infant daughter of Z.W. & M. (August 30, 1918)
27. Brown, James G. (January 8, 1881–August 26, 1919)
28. Brown, Lydia A. (February 5, 1865–February 22, 1913)
29. Brown, Sudie Womble (June 13, 1885–October 10, 1958)[10]
30. Brown, Virginia (no dates)
31. Bulliner, David (July 4, 1814–February 9, 1899)
32. Bulliner, David A., son of G.W. & Nancy Bulliner (died March 30, 1874, aged 25 years, 6 months, and 16 days)
33. Bulliner, Elizabeth, wife of David Bulliner (March 12, 1837–July 2, 1904)
34. Bulliner, George W. (died December 12, 1873, aged 61 years, 10 months, and 9 days)
35. Bulliner, Martha A. (January 9, 1848–April 11, 1864)
36. Bulliner, Micajah, son of D. & E. Bulliner (September 25, 1879–August 26, 1902)
37. Bulliner, Nancy, wife of G.W. Bulliner (died August 10, 1880, aged 58 years, 6 months, and 4 days)
38. Bulliner, Nancy (1818–December 1, 1877)
39. Bulliner, Rebecca (1789–October 19, 1855)
40. Bulliner, Sudie, daughter of G.W. & Jennie Bulliner (August 11, 1871–April 25, 1874)
41. Burkeen, George Thomas (January 15, 1882–July 19, 1943)
42. Burkeen, Parlee Robison (February 27, 1893–August 11, 1963)
43. Burkeens, Fay Marie, daughter of G.T. & E.P. Burkeens (June 14, 1926–August 9, 1927)

7. Tommy Boyd was an itinerant artist known for painting signs. He painted many landscapes on buildings.

8. Buddie died at the age of seven years; he was a frail child and very sickly. He attended the Possom Trot Schoolhouse and his appearance in a group photograph shows that he is very sick already in 1897.

9. Cornelius Brown, often referred to as "Nēlus" Brown, was the father of Zanie Brown and grandfather of Guy Brown and Mary Frances Brown Robison. His second wife was Ms. Virginia "Ginny" Brown.

10. Sudie Womble Brown was the daughter of Thomas J. Womble and the wife of Iley Brown.

44. Burkeens, Uneeda May (May 21, 1922–July 20, 1924)
45. Carroll, H.W. (October 31, 1846–September 24, 1919)[11]
46. Carroll, Lenora J. (1883–1966)[12]
47. Carroll, Lucindia C. (1872–1951)
48. Carroll, M.V., daughter of H.W. & M.A. Carroll (December 29, 1878–October 28, 1879)
49. Carroll, Mary, wife of H.W. Carroll (March 13, 1851–April 1, 1927)
50. Case, J.D. (1846–1934)
51. Case, Joan, wife of J.D. Case (1853–1913)
52. Catron-Hambrick, Christopher Sean (October 14, 1989–April 4, 1999)
53. Clayton, France (1841–1925)[13]
54. Clayton, Nicy B., wife of John B. Clayton (March 25, 1854–February 21, 1873)
55. Clayton, infant daughter of John B. & Nicy B. (February 21, 1873)
56. Clayton, Jesse (unmarked)
57. Clayton, Mary C., wife of Robert M. Clayton (born circa 1835–?)
    Although there is no specific record for the burial of Mary C. Clayton in Mount Carmel, there is no record for her burial elsewhere either. Further, the tombstone belonging to Robert M. Clayton and daughter Permelia J. Clayton is a four sided obelisk and one side is not graven but rather unmarked. Still further, there is a grave on that side where Mary C. Clayton otherwise would have been buried. It is believed by the author that Mary C. Clayton occupies that grave.
58. Clayton, Permelia J., daughter of Robert M. Clayton (born January 31, 1860, aged 6 years)
59. Clayton, Robert M. (February 17, 1827–January 14, 1863)[14]
60. Cogdell, Elmer Louis (February 3, 1923–April 8, 2012)

11. Carroll's first name was Hugh.

12. Lenora and Lucindia Carroll are the sisters often referred to as Cindy and Nora Carroll. At one point, they lived in the old home that later became Wilson's Grocery. That site is now the Finger Grocery Store site on Highway 199 near the current Finger Post Office.

13. France Clayton was a veteran of the Confederate Army having served a private in Company F of the Thirteenth Tennessee Infantry

14. Robert M. Clayton was a member of the McNairy County Quarterly Court.

61. Cogdell, Nancy Virginia, wife of Elmer Cogdell (November 13, 1923–July 11, 1989)[15]
62. Coleman, I.J. (May 18, 1825–August 20, 1891)[16]
63. Covey, Mary A., wife of C.B. Covey (January 6, 1833–January 24, 1893)[17]
64. Covy, Charles B. (December 6, 1823–November 22, 1862)[18]
65. Covy, infant son of C.B. & M.A. (no dates)
66. Crowe, C.G., son of M.T. & W.S. Crowe (August 8, 1903–November 10, 1903)
67. Crowe, William Sherman, son of W.S. & Mary T, Crowe (November 13, 1901–January 10, 1905)
68. Cude, Lydia J., wife of N.W. Cude (December 4, 1860–May 8, 1884)
69. Davis, Allie B. (1908–1968)
70. Davis, Arl E. (June 29, 1914–June 30, 2008)
71. Davis, Jessie N. (November 20, 1917–May 26, 1999)[19]
72. Davis, Louise (December 16, 1935–February 1936)
73. Davis, Michael (January 22, 1950–September 6, 1956)
74. Deaton, James Ervin (1879–1950)
75. Deaton, Minnie Lee, wife of J.E. Deaton (1880–1967)
76. Dempsey, Malisa A. (November 4, 1876–September 19, 1904)[20]
77. Dickey, John R., son of G.W. & A.E. Dickey (December 21, 1871–September 20, 1873)[21]
78. Draper, Mrs. (died in 1887) *Unmarked*[22]

15. Nancy Virginia Cogdell was the daughter of A.M. McCann and wife Celia McCann.

16. I.J. Coleman is referred to as both Isabel J. Coleman and Isabella J. Coleman in this work.

17. Mary A. Covey was the daughter of Jacob Lowrance and Susanah Lowrance.

18. Covey served as a sergeant in the U.S. Sixth Tennessee Cavalry and died during his service.

19. Jessie N. Davis was the daughter of A.M. McCann and wife Celia McCann. She was married to Arl E. Davis. Louise and Michael Davis, buried nearby, were their children.

20. The author is uncertain if Malisa A. Dempsey is the only member of the Dempsey family buried at Mt. Carmel. The farm in the vicinity of the "Rock Pile" was known as the "Dempsey place." It is likely that other members of the Dempsey family are buried here as well.

21. This is the son of George W. Dickey and wife Amanda E. McIntyre Dickey, the grandson of Robert Thompson McIntyre and Sarah Jane Weaver McIntyre, and the brother of Ophelia Dickey, Doll Dickey, Freelin Dickey, and others.

22. Mrs. Draper's burial at Mount Carmel was reported by the *American Wesleyan*.

79. English, Myrtle Beene, wife of Lee English (1890–1934)[23]
80. Floyd, infant son of W.E. & Jewell (born & died March 3, 1930)
81. Floyd, Ben A. (November 3, 1892–December 25, 1943)[24]
82. Floyd, Effie, daughter of I.P. & S.L. Floyd (Died October 9, 1911, at age 13 of typhoid fever and was attended by Dr. Nathaniel A. Tucker of Finger, Tennessee)[25]
83. Floyd, I.P. (December 7, 1867–April 15, 1941)
84. Floyd, Ida, daughter of I.P. & S.L. Floyd (no dates)
85. Floyd, Lydia, daughter of I.P. & S.L. Floyd (no dates)
86. Floyd, Sarah L., wife of I.P. Floyd (September 6, 1870–February 26, 1959)
87. Floyd, William E. (July 8, 1910–April 2, 1982)[26]
88. Fowler, Nancy Plunk (May 27, 1847–November 25, 1925) Daughter of George and Fannie Gorman Plunk. This is an unmarked grave.[27]
89. Gage, the grandfather of Wash (no dates)
90. Gibson, Thomas Leonard (August 18, 1938–December 17, 2003)
91. Green, Linda Charlene (May 21, 1953–September 2, 2005)
92. Griffin, Charlie B. (March 28, 1890–December 14, 1964)
93. Griffin, Eunice, daughter of J.W. & Ophelia Griffin (August 5, 1913–October 15, 1915)
94. Griffin, J.W. (July 8, 1888–May 4, 1971)
95. Griffin, Ludie W. (July 15, 1894–February 8, 1988)
96. Griffin, M.E., wife of J.A. Griffin (September 21, 1878–October 31, 1900)
97. Griffin, Sara Ophelia, wife of J.W. Griffin (January 2, 1884–April 13, 1960)
98. Griswell, Louisa Rebecca (born in July 1860)

23. According to some contemporary sources (including the late Lessie McIntyre), Myrtle Beene English died in the mental institution in Bolivar, Tennessee. Myrtle Beene English was the daughter of William Moses and Melissa (Coleman) Beene.

24. Ben A. Floyd was a good friend and school chum of James Orby Massey.

25. *McNairy County, Tennessee Death Book, 1908-1912.* McNairy County Records Commission.

26. William E. Floyd's grave lies beneath a double tombstone with his wife, Jewell B. Floyd. Following her death, Jewell B. Floyd chose to be buried in the Old Friendship Cemetery on Old Friendship Road with members of her family. She was born in 1908 and died in 2010, well past the age of 100 years.

27. Nancy Wardlow Kennedy, compiler. *Unmarked Graves in McNairy County, Tennessee*, Selmer, TN: Self-published, 2006.

99. Griswell, Mary M. (L.) (April 1873–July 1, 1928)[28]
100. Guinn, Cayce Allen (born & died 1996)
101. Hair, Prince E., son of J.C. & M.E. Hair (August 23, 1882–June 29, 1883)
102. Halstead, Emily F. (January 24, 1843–September 29, 1924)
103. Halstead, John W. (September 26, 1879–February 27, 1917)
104. Halstead, Taylor (1850–1894)
105. Hand, Minnie Irene Plunk (May 19, 1896–May 19, 1921) Daughter of Alfred Plunk and Kizzie Dunn Plunk
106. Harris, Allie B. (no dates)
107. Harris, Augustus (1876–1930)
108. Harris, Doris, daughter of J.R. & Ora Harris (October 28, 1905–January 15, 1906)[29]
109. Harris, Earnest, son of J.J. & N.C. Harris (May 21, 1884–April 16, 1885)
110. Harris, Emma, wife of T.G. Harris (April 3, 1875–March 3, 1905)
111. Harris, Fannie (1882–1971)
112. Harris, Henry C. (June 11, 1844–October 10, 1917)[30]
113. Harris, James J. (1851–1930)
114. Harris, Jimmie (February 4, 1873–February 17, 1942)
115. Harris, Joanna, wife of N.A. Harris (February 27, 1844–March 2, 1913)
116. Harris, N.A. (April 20, 1838–February 10, 1916)[31]
117. Harris, Nancy A., wife of Henry C. Harris (April 21, 1850–May 1, 1936)[32]

28. The Federal Census for McNairy County listed Griswell's birth year as April 1873, but Gooch Funeral Home Records indicate that she was sixty-four years old at the time of her death, placing her birth year as 1864.

29. John R. Harris is buried with his second wife, Zaida McCaskill Harris, at Old Friendship Cemetery near Finger, and Ora Lee Harris is buried in the Adamsville City Cemetery in Adamsville, Tennessee.

30. Henry Clay Harris was a private in Company B of the U.S. Sixth Tennessee Cavalry, having enlisted on August 25, 1862, and being mustered into service on November 13, 1862. However, according to Dr. Alicia Wilkerson, Henry first joined the Confederate Army and fought at the Battle of Pittsburg Landing (Shiloh) and then three months afterward, he joined the United States (Union) Army.

31. Nathan A. Harris and wife Joanna Harris were the parents of Bliss Harris (1876–1963).

32. Nancy Adeline Barham was the daughter of Thomas M. Barham and wife Margaret Amanda "Peggy" Blakely Barham. She married Henry Clay Harris on November 22, 1868, with William L. Cockram officiating.

118. Harris, Nancy C., wife of James J. Harris (1850–?)
119. Harris, Pinkney A., son of Arthur & Lucy Harris (May 31, 1853–August 11, 1890)
120. Harris, T.G. (March 27, 1866–December 9, 1954)
121. Harris, W.A., son of J.J. & N.C. Harris, September 14, 1872–February 25, 1917)
122. Heathcock, Robert L. Jr. (July 15, 1946–August 28, 2005)
123. Hendrix, Mary Uda, daughter of Mr. & Mrs. A.H. Hendrix (September 10, 1894–November 19, 1894)
124. Hill, Larry C. (1949–1984)
125. Hodges, infant of Horry & M.E. (January 8, 1863–January 11, 1863)
126. Hodges, infant of Horry & M.E. (January 8, 1863–January 11, 1863)[33]
127. Hodges, Elijah J., captain of the Sixth Tennessee Cavalry, U.S.A. (May 18, 1831–April 21, 1913)
128. Hodges, Harmon E. (December 3, 1871–November 17, 1957)
129. Hodges, Harvey G. (March 17, 1878–September 1, 1922)
130. Hodges, Horry (March 19, 1868–September 23, 1940)
131. Hodges, James Wright (August 28, 1857–November 8, 1916)[34]
132. Hodges, Jane, wife of E.J. Hodges (September 22, 1834–September 8, 1921)
133. Hodges, John, son of E.J. & N.J. Hodges (January 27, 1862–April 18, 1862)
134. Hodges, Julia Ann (1878–1958)[35]
135. Hodges, Maggie (March 27, 1876–October 30, 1955)
136. Hodges, Mary Elizabeth, wife of James W. Hodges (January 2, 1859–February 4, 1936)

33. These were twin infants who were born during Captain Horry Hodges' service in the War Between the States.

34. James Wright Hodges was the son of Captain Horry Hodges and Sarah Elizabeth Dodd Hodges. He married Mary Elizabeth James Hodges and the couple had four children: Julia Ann Hodges, William Horry Hodges, Hugh L. Hodges, and John Edgar Hodges.

35. Julia "Julie" Ann Hodges was a spinster who taught school in her youth and later ran a boarding house across the road from the Finger School. Her home was located next to that of Dr. W.M. Barnes and still stands today. She was known for having a somewhat stern and sour temperament. According to local merchant Thee Harris, if one saw Julie Hodges and her stockings were pulled tight and straight, her mood was tolerable and could even border on pleasant if required. However, Harris said that if her stockings were twisted, crooked, and generally bad fitting, then it was, "Watch out, brother, because Julie was on a tear!"

137. Hodges, Sarah Ann, daughter of E.J. & N.J. Hodges (August 24, 1857–July 27, 1858)

138. Hodges, Tabitha F., daughter of E.J. & N.J. Hodges (December 28, 1854–August 29, 1855)

139. Hodges, Dr. William Henry (September 19, 1869–November 16, 1941)

140. Holland, Jennie Sipes, wife of W.C. Holland (1868–1924)[36]

141. Hubanks, Annie (February 15, 1894–October 1, 1947)

142. Hubanks, Dave (February 12, 1857–August 16, 1924)

143. Hubanks, Erleana (1890–1906)

144. Hubanks, J.L. (January 6, 1846–January 1, 1915)[37]

145. Hubanks, J.L.P., son of J.L. & Susan Hubanks (June 5, 1880–July 17, 1880)[38]

146. Hubanks, J.L. Posey, son of J.L. & Susan Hubanks (June 5, 1880–July 27, 1880)

147. Hubanks, Jennie (1864–1904)

148. Hubanks, John Shelley (September 20, 1898–October 18, 1982)[39]

149. Hubanks, Ruffie N. (1901–1906)

150. Hubanks, Sam J. (January 19, 1893–June 18, 1979)

151. Hubanks, Susan, wife of J.L. Hubanks (January 20, 1843–June 21, 1913)

152. Hubanks, W.B. (July 19, 1847–April 24, 1938)

153. Hubanks, William Barney (October 6, 1896–March 28, 1994)

154. James, Mary J., daughter of J.H. & S.I. James (September 8, 1862–July 1864)

36. Jennie Ann (Sipes) Holland was born in McNairy County on August 12, 1870, the daughter of Powell and Sallie (Gage) Sipes. She was the second wife of William Columbus Holland, who is buried at Liberty Church Cemetery beside his first wife, Charlotte (McCann) Holland. Jennie contracted influenza and died on March 5, 1924, and her husband succumbed to the same illness just "51 hours and 30 minutes" afterward, according to their obituary. Her funeral service was performed at Mount Carmel by Rev. Eber Smith. Jennie Ann Hollins [Holland] Death Certificate No. 109. Tennessee Death Records, 1914–1955. <familysearch.org>. *McNairy County Independent*, March 28, 1924.

37. It is believed that J.L. Hubanks' mother, Ellen Hubanks (also known as Ellen Eubanks), is buried at Mount Carmel next to Robert Thompson McIntyre. She was McIntyre's second wife. Her two daughters are also likely buried next to her.

38. J.L.P. Hubanks and J.L. Posey Hubanks are most likely the same child, not twins.

39. Shelley, Sam, and Barney Hubanks were bachelor brothers who lived together and divided their housekeeping, gardening, and farming chores amongst themselves. Barney Hubanks was very financially supportive of Mount Carmel Cemetery.

155. James, Nancy A., wife of William R. James (November 15, 1838–September 15, 1923)
156. Johnson, John (1826–June 22, 1876)
157. Johnson, Ewin (1822–March 30, 1857)
158. Johnson, Joannah E. (April 13, 1850–February 2, 1875)
159. Johnson, Margaret E. (March 5, 1852–October 7, 1861)
160. Johnson, Mary J. (July 18, 1853–April 14, 1873)
161. Johnson, N.S.C. (1853–March 12, 1876)
162. Jones, Callie E., daughter of C.C. & M.J. Jones (September 22, 1881–March 10, 1895)
163. Jones, John R. (October 8, 1886–November 13, 1909)[40]
164. Jones, Mary Alabama (October 30, 1855–March 19, 1903)
165. Joyner, Thomas Arley (March 6, 1912–December 12, 1959)
166. Kaufman, Ava Lee (September 1, 1931–August 26, 2004)[41]
167. Keel, Martha Plunk (1879–1908)
168. Kerby, Alonzo (1858–1862) Son of Hugh and Martha Kerby; unmarked grave[42]
169. Kerby, Hugh (1821–1870)
170. Kerby, Martha J. Hendrix, wife of Hugh Kerby (February 11, 1830–July 3, 1864)
171. Kinney, Alice Mae (April 19, 1928–August 25, 2007)[43]
172. Kinney, Edward D. (March 26, 1926–January 9, 2005)
173. Kinney, Thomas E. (March 15, 1953–December 6, 1991)
174. Kirkpatrick, Betsy (1841–1932)
175. Kirkpatrick, Catherine A. (1888–1970)[44]
176. Kirkpatrick, Charlie Hugh (August 8, 1830–February 6, 1907)
177. Kirkpatrick, Elbert A. (October 27, 1914–March 11, 1985)[45]

40. The sadness of the Jones' family at John R. Jones' death was summed up with his epitaph, "How many hopes lie buried here."

41. Ava Lee Kaufman was one of the many children of Arthur Marion Douglas "Whig" McCann and Celia (Weaver) McCann.

42. Kennedy, *Unmarked Graves in McNairy County, Tennessee*.

43. Alice Mae Kinney was the daughter of John T. "Jack" Kirkpatrick and wife Catherine (Weaver) Kirkpatrick.

44. Catherine A. Weaver Kirkpatrick was the daughter of Absalom Weaver Jr. and the sister of Celia (Weaver) McCann.

45. Elbert A. Kirkpatrick was a son of John T. "Jack" Kirkpatrick and wife Catherine A. (Weaver) Kirkpatrick.

178. Kirkpatrick, Eliza (1822–circa 1855) *Unmarked grave*[46]

179. Kirkpatrick, John T. (1877–1953)

180. Kirkpatrick, Martha Ann Barham (December 19, 1837–August 23, 1915)

181. Kirkpatrick, Mollie Bell (1874–1949)

182. Kirkpatrick, W.E. (August 7, 1832–January 4, 1913)[47]

183. Kiser, Harlie W. (January 31, 1922–[July 27] 1986) *PFC, U.S. Army, World War II*

184. Kiser, Opal, wife of H.W. Kiser (February 28, 1924–August 13, 1984)

185. Lain, Amanda C., wife of A.C. Lain (April 22, 1850–September 19, 1878)

186. Lain, Araminta, daughter of J.S. & N.E. Lain, (January 27, 1878–August 6, 1889)

187. Lain, Hugh M., son of J.S. & N.E. Lain (October 29, 1867–June 30, 1868)

188. Lain, J.S. (December 2, 1845–May 29, 1932)[48]

189. Lain, Jane A., wife of Thomas Lain (March 17, 1821–August 25, 1871)

190. Lain, John H., son of Thomas & Jane Lain (July 16, 1840–November 11, 1855)

191. Lain, Lillie Amandy, daughter of A.C. & M.G. Lain (July 13, 1878–February 11, 1903)

192. Lain, Mary Ollie, daughter of A.C. & Mattie Lain (June 15, 1888–June 30, 1897)

193. Lain, Mattie, wife of A.C. Lain (1850–1942)

194. Lain, Maudie, daughter of J.S. & N.E. Lain (August 10, 1886–March 23, 1911)

195. Lain, Nancy E., wife of J.S. Lain (January 10, 1850–November 10, 1935)[49]

196. Lain, Nannie C., wife of W.M. Lain (January 21, 1858–January 29, 1889)

46. Kennedy, *Unmarked Graves in McNairy County, Tennessee.*

47. His given name was William Elijah Kirkpatrick.

48. James Simpson Lain, the son of Thomas and Janie (Wilson) Lain (both of whom are also buried at Mount Carmel), was a local farmer and justice of the peace. James Simpson Lain Death Certificate No. 10422. Tennessee Death Records, 1914–1955. <familysearch.org>

49. Nancy Elizabeth Lain was the daughter of Hugh Kerby.

197. Lain, Reuben G., son of Thomas & Jane A. Lain (August 22, 1856–
     August 12, 1876)
198. Lain, Sarah A., wife of W.M. Lain (August 4, 1854–February 27, 1878)
199. Lain, Susan V. Rhodes, wife of W.M. Lain (November 23, 1865–July
     29, 1938)
200. Lain, Thomas (March 15, 1807–November 15, 1886)[50]
201. Lain, W.M. (April 20, 1848–March 2, 1903)
202. Lane, A.C. (August 20, 1850–October 29, 1904)
203. Livingston, Josephine L., wife of G.W. Livingston (June 17, 1859–
     July 16, 1888)
204. Lofton, Rosie (died 1906)[51]
205. Long, James (February 10, 1845–August 21, 1914) *Son of Reuben Long
     and Martha Jewell Long*
206. Long, Susan A. Ferguson, wife of James Long (July 28, 1856–July
     9, 1949)
207. Loudermilk, Eldridge Wayne (May 20, 1934–August 26, 1991)
208. Lowrance, Abram (died 1826) *Unmarked*
209. Lowrance, Jacob (April 20, 1803–August 11, 1882)
210. Lowrance, John L., son of J.M. & H.E. Lowrance (March 28, 1872–
     November 9, 1873)
211. Lowrance, Susana, wife of Jacob Lowrance (October 14, 1814–April
     19, 1837)[52]
212. Lowery, child of Adam and Margaret (Doss) Lowery *Unmarked*[53]
213. Lowery, child of Adam and Margaret (Doss) Lowery *Unmarked*
214. Lowery, child of Adam and Margaret (Doss) Lowery *Unmarked*
215. Macon, Elijah (Died September 27, 1867, aged 57 years, 1 month,
     and 14 days)[54]
216. Macon, Honor, wife of Elijah Macon (January 20, 1812–March 6, 1898)

50. Thomas Lain was from North Carolina and an early settler of north McNairy County.

51. Rosie Lofton died in childbirth. She was the maternal grandmother of Troy Moore of Selmer, Tennessee. She died giving birth to his mother.

52. Susana Lowrance is the first known marked grave. It is possible that an earlier marker or markers once existed in the center portion of the graveyard before it was destroyed when that area was logged to harvest its cedars.

53. The three Lowrey children were the siblings of Confederate Brigadier General Mark Perrin Lowrey.

54. Although it cannot be verified currently, it is believed that Elijah Macon's father, Thomas Macon, who died in 1866 in McNairy County, Tennessee, is buried in Mt. Carmel Cemetery.

217. Maness, Dovy Honor, daughter of R.G. & Missouri Maness (July 5, 1877–July 27, 1877)

218. Maness, George Thomas, son of R.G. & Missouri Maness (September 25, 1874–November 29, 1874)

219. Maness, Melitia, wife of George R. Maness (February 4, 1848–February 14, 1871)

220. Mason, James (July 1, 1804–June 14, 1880)

221. Mason, Priscilla, wife of James Mason (January 13, 1814–July 20, 1888)

222. Massey, Beulah O., daughter of W.P. & S.L. Massey (March 20, 1901–May 4, 1904)[55]

223. Massey, C.E., wife of W.P. Massey (September 17, 1866–February 2, 1890)[56]

224. Massey, Cyrathia A., daughter of D.P. & S.E. Massey (October 6, 1862–December 11, 1863)

225. Massey, D.P. (March 15, 1834–September 25, 1870)[57]

226. Massey, Sarah E., wife of D.P. Massey (September 5, 1843–March 28, 1869)[58]

227. Massey, Sarah J., daughter of D.P. & S.E. Massey (August 4, 1865–December 23, 1870)

228. McCann, A.D. (June 16, 1910–August 4, 1964)[59]

229. McCann, A.M. (April 11, 1859–August 24, 1937)

230. McCann, Arthur C. (May 25, 1883–July 10, 1962)[60]

231. McCann, Betty Jane (August 10, 1939–April 9, 1940)[61]

232. McCann, Billy Joe, son of Marion H. & Dahlia McCann (born & died August 6, 1934)

55. The majority of the W.P. and Saphronia Massey family is buried in the Finger Cemetery.

56. Nothing is really known of C.E. Massey, the first wife of W.P. Massey. However, the author believes W.P. Massey's first wife was Cora L. Haynie (Haynes), and that the couple was married on October 15, 1889.

57. David Pinkney Massey was the son of Thomas Massey.

58. Sarah E. Massey was the daughter of Robert Thompson McIntyre and Sarah Jane Weaver McIntyre.

59. A.D. McCann was the son of Arthur Marion Douglas and Celia (Weaver) McCann.

60. Arthur Columbus "Arter" McCann was the son of Arthur Marion Douglas and Parthenia (Tacker) McCann.

61. Betty Jane McCann was the daughter of A.D. and Annie (Shirley) McCann.

233. McCann, Celia W., wife of A.M. McCann (September 20, 1892–January 22, 1968)[62]
234. McCann, Dell (January 3, 1916–May 20, 1999)
235. McCann, Elsie, wife of W.A. McCann (August 6, 1886–January 22, 1958)
236. McCann, Hazel (born & died February 8, 1928)[63]
237. McCann, Mary A. (1909–1927)[64]
238. McCann, Nora W., wife of A.D. McCann (December 23, 1911–May 18, 1973)
239. McCann, Ola (June ___ 1914–June 1, 1928)[65]
240. McCann, Pearl, daughter of W.A. & E.A. McCann (September 9, 1908–July 29, 1916)
241. McCann, R.B. (born & died 1919)[66]
242. McCann, Rex Adell, infant son of Dell & Fay McCann (born & died August 2, 1949)
243. McCann, Truman (December 30, 1880–March 5, 1948)[67]
244. McCann, Verdie R., daughter of W.A. & Elsie McCann (October 24, 1922- May 29, 1925)
245. McCann, W.A. (January 1, 1886- August 1, 1970)[68]
246. McHolstead, Elizabeth S., wife of W.A. McHolstead (November 25, 1809–March 17, 1886)
247. McHolstead, Reverend W.A. (November 11, 1806–March 23, 1891)

62. Celia W. McCann was the daughter of Absalom Weaver Jr. and the sister of Catherine A. Kirkpatrick. Her first name was actually Cordelia, but she was called "Celia" (pronounced by her family as "Celie").

63. Hazel McCann was the infant daughter of Arthur Marion Douglas and Celia (Weaver) McCann.

64. Mary A. McCann was the daughter of Truman and Ila (Womble) McCann.

65. Ola McCann was the daughter of Arthur Marion Douglas and Celia (Weaver) McCann. She died at about 14 years old as the result of bumping heads with her younger sister Beulah McCann.

66. R.B. McCann was the infant son of Truman and Ila (Womble) McCann.

67. Truman Pleasant McCann was born on December 30, 1880, the son of Arthur Marion Douglas "Whig" McCann and wife Parthenia Tacker McCann. Truman attended school at Lain's Academy. While still a young man, probably about thirty, Truman was injured while plowing. He was plowing and a sharp root was plowed up and cut his leg. Infection set in and his leg had to be amputated. The leg is buried near him under an unmarked stone. He became a photographer and later ran a hamburger stand.

68. William Andrew "Ander" McCann was the son of Arthur Marion Douglas and Parthenia (Tacker) McCann.

248. McIntyre, Audrey Roberta (November 19, 1928–September 25, 1935)[69]
249. McIntyre, B.A., son of J.R. & M.R. McIntyre (December 26, 1874–January 3, 1877)
250. McIntyre, Elizabeth (Died January 8, 1858, aged 78 years)
251. McIntyre, Fannie E. Carroll, wife of James R. McIntyre (December 13, 1874–August 6, 1950)[70]
252. McIntyre, Henry, son of J.R. & M.R. McIntyre (September 8, 1891–September 10, 1891)
253. McIntyre, Hubert U. (1897–1976)[71]
254. McIntyre, Infant son of Mr. & Mrs. U.H. (born & died 1926)
255. McIntyre, Infant son of J.R. & M.R. (born & died August 25, 1870)
256. McIntyre, Isac T., son of J.R. & M.R. McIntyre (December 15, 1880–December 17, 1880)
257. McIntyre, John Absalom (April 27, 1848–November 6, 1897)
258. McIntyre, James E., son of R.A. & S.F. McIntyre (May 5, 1899–October 4, 1900)[72]
259. McIntyre, James R. (November 29, 1849–December 30, 1921)
260. McIntyre, John J., son of J.R. & M.R. McIntyre (March 28, 1882–November 7, 1883)
261. McIntyre, John Robert (July 27, 1893–September 19, 1989)[73]
262. McIntyre, Lessie (December 25, 1914–January 2, 2005)
263. McIntyre, Lula Womble (May 23, 1890–October 9, 1966)
264. McIntyre, Maggie L., wife of H.U. McIntyre (1898–1973)[74]

69. Audrey Roberta McIntyre was the daughter of Hubert and Maggie McIntyre. She died of diphtheria at the age of six years.

70. Mrs. Fannie Carroll McIntyre was a native of the Adamsville, Tennessee area.

71. Hubert McIntyre was a World War I era veteran. To the author's knowledge, he served stateside.

72. R.A. McIntyre, the father of James E. McIntyre, was Robert Allen McIntyre, the son of James Robert McIntyre and grandson of Robert Thompson McIntyre.

73. John Robert McIntyre, the son of John Absalom McIntyre and Mary Robert Coleman McIntyre, was trained as a machinist in Corinth, Mississippi, farmed, and made custom brooms in his shop with his wife, Ollie Pearl McCann McIntyre, who was the daughter of Arthur Marion Douglas "Whig" McCann and wife Parthenia Tacker McCann. McIntyre was known for his ability to build things and tinker with items in efforts to make them work better.

74. Mrs. Maggie McIntyre was a sister to A. Tucker Robison and Lawrence "Red" Robison.

265. McIntyre, Margaret R., wife of James R. McIntyre (November 7, 1851–November 16, 1904)[75]

266. McIntyre, Mary Helen (July 2, 1912–November 8, 1962)

267. McIntyre, Nancy Caroline, daughter of R.T. McIntyre (October 14, 1852–October 7, 1855)

268. McIntyre, Ollie Pearl, wife of John R. McIntyre (October 7, 1894–February 19, 1980)

269. McIntyre, Robert Thompson (May 28, 1814–November 7, 1902)

270. McIntyre, Rachel, daughter of J.R. & Fannie McIntyre (December 25, 1910–January 28, 1914)

271. McIntyre, Robertie M., wife of J.A. McIntyre (February 28, 1860–November 8, 1907)[76]

272. McIntyre, Sarah F., wife of R.A. McIntyre (February 20, 1873–April 2, 1900)

273. McIntyre, Sarah Jane, wife of R.T. McIntyre (August 7, 1820–January 12, 1875)[77]

274. McIntyre, Vergie I., daughter of J.R. & M.R. McIntyre (December 9, 1878–July 28, 1898)[78]

275. McIntyre, Vivian (November 28, 1921–November 13, 2004)

276. McIntyre, Zenar, daughter of J.A. & M.R. McIntyre (February 15, 1883–December 6, 1907)[79]

277. McVay, Carl T. (1909–1971)

278. McVay, Eula E., wife of Carl T. McVay (1909–2000)

279. McVay, Johnie Mildred (born & died 1928)

---

75. Margaret Rebecca McIntyre was the daughter of Allen Louis Beene and Mary Jane Beene.

76. Her actual name was Mary Roberta (Coleman) McIntyre.

77. Sarah Jane McIntyre was the daughter of Absalom Weaver, Sr. and the aunt of Celia McCann and Catherine A. Kirkpatrick.

78. Vergie I. McIntyre was a very attractive and talented young lady. She died prior to her twentieth birthday. According to Betty Sitton Reed, Vergie was a talented painter and left behind at least one beautiful piece of artwork, a painting of a horse that eventually came into the possession of her half-sister, Ruth Moore.

79. Zenar McIntyre was a victim of the 1907 typhoid fever breakout in the north McNairy County area. At the time of her death, she was said to be engaged to a fellow by the name of Bedford Cone. According to family tradition, Mr. Cone was not in the area when Zenar died. When Cone read the letter informing him of Zenar's death, his tears fell and streaked and smeared the ink on the letter.

280. Miller, Esbell (Isbell) Fowler, Mother of R. Jenkins Miller and wife of Isaac Miller, born circa 1842–date of death unknown.[80]
281. Miller, R. Jenkins (June 19, 1870–August 16, 1951)[81]
282. Nash, General B. *Unmarked*[82]
283. Owen, David F. (March 14, 1810–June 24, 1889)
284. Owen, J.N. (1876–1952)[83]
285. Owen, Mary E., wife W.R. Owen (October 25, 1883–July 4, 1901)
286. Owen, Mary Elizabeth (no dates)[84]
287. Owen, Mary Jane, wife of J.N. Owen (1877–1955)
288. Owen, Mary S., daughter of W.R. & M.A. Owen (October 16, 1873–September 16, 1897)
289. Owen, R.H. (September 20, 1870–August 5, 1898)
290. Owen, W.R. (December 13, 1835–June 9, 1914) Although this is a marked grave, the same individual appears to be enumerated as an unmarked grave in an index of unmarked graves in McNairy County and is listed as Robert W. Owen (December 14, 1834–June 9, 1914), son of David Owen.
291. Ozment, T.H. (1846–1913)
292. Pace, C.P. (March 5, 1881–October 12, 1958)
293. Pace, Clara Stanfill, wife of C.P. Pace (August 11, 1902–March 8, 1942)
294. Pace, Hassie Mae, daughter of C.P. Pace (August 27, 1911–March 3, 1912)
295. Pace, James Leroy (February 17, 1913–January 9, 1948)
296. Pace, Luzena, wife of C.P. Pace (July 7, 1888–January 31, 1934)

80. Her son R. Jenkins "Red" Miller's death certificate gives her name as Esbell (Fowler) Miller. However, Elizabeth Fowler married Isham Miller in McNairy County around August 22, 1870.

81. R. Jenkins "Red" Miller was the son of Issac and Esbell (Fowler) Miller. He was a well-known local hobo who never married. He was reputed to have traveled throughout the 48 contiguous states and Canada and Mexico. He was a peculiar fellow, but remained beloved by many in the community. When he died at the McNairy County Poorhouse in Selmer, Tennessee on August 16, 1951, they got together and helped pay for Miller's tombstone.

82. Nash was the grandfather or great-grandfather of the late Robert Nash of Finger, Tennessee.

83. Jasper Newton "Nute" Owen was a farmer and merchant in the McNairy Station area.

84. Mary Elizabeth Owen was born on April 8, 1904, and died on December 7, 1991.

297. Patterson, infant son of Allen & Mary Patterson (born & died October 20, 1914) *Unmarked grave*[85]

298. Patterson, Allen (no date)[86]

299. Patterson, Mary (no dates)[87]

300. Peeples, Bettie, wife of W.W. Peeples (1860–1939)[88]

301. Peeples, Charles Banner (December 19, 1868–March 17, 1951)[89]

302. Peeples, John C. (1872–August 18, 1949)

303. Peeples, Mary Jane "Molly" (1865–March 8, 1952)

304. Peeples, Nancy C. (August 4, 1839–March 9, 1917)[90]

305. Peeples, W.W. (November 29, 1850–February 16, 1904)

306. Phillips, Charles Franklin, son of Tennie Starks (February 1, 1924–April 1, 2002)

307. Plunk, infant of D.F. (born & died 1913)

308. Plunk, infant of J.M. & wife

309. Plunk, infant of J.M. & wife

310. Plunk, Alfred Monroe (1836–1918) *Son of George Plunk*[91]

311. Plunk, David F. (1885–1976)

---

85. Unnamed Patterson Death Certificate No. 153. Tennessee Death Records 1914–1955. <familysearch.org>. The certificate indicates the premature baby was buried at Mount Carmel, Bishop & O'Neal of Finger, undertakers.

86. Allen Patterson was a well-known drunkard who lived in the Finger area. Regardless, he was still well-liked by many.

87. Mary Francis (Ramey) Patterson's death certificate gives her dates as (May 18, 1881–July 8, 1932). She was the wife of Allen Patterson and the daughter of Bert and Elizabeth (Estes) Ramey. Mary Francis Patterson Death Certificate No. 14964. Tennessee Death Records, 1914–1955. <familysearch.org>

88. Bettie Peeples was the daughter of Captain Elijah J. Hodges and wife Nancy Jane Dodd Hodges and the sister of Harvey, Horry, Henry, Harmon and Maggie Hodges.

89. Banner Peeples, John C. Peeples, and Mary Jane "Molly" Peeples were all siblings. John C. Peeples was married to Annie Talbott.

90. Nancy C. Peeples appears to have been Nancy C. Barham, the wife of J.B. Peeples. The couple married on March 1, 1862, with Justice of the Peace Nathan Barnes officiating and J.B. Harris acting as bondsman.

91. Alfred Monroe Plunk was also known as Alford Monroe Plunk. He first married Emily Caroline Dickey, the daughter of John A. Dickey and wife Sarah Dickey, on November 25, 1869, with the Reverend Wilson A. McHolstead officiating. He married Kizzie Dunn on or about December 17, 1879. Her father, John Dunn, served as the bondsman for this marriage.

312. Plunk, E. Lawson (October 22, 1870–August 1, 1909)[92]

313. Plunk, Elisha L. (December 27, 1824–March 17, 1911) *Died of dysentery while being treated by Dr. Nathaniel A. Tucker.*[93]

314. Plunk, Emily Dickey (1844–1879)

315. Plunk, H.J., child of S.C. & L.A. Plunk (March 21, 1877–July 20, 1879)

316. Plunk, Kizzie Dunn (1850–1925)[94]

317. Plunk, L.A., wife of S.C. Plunk (August 29, 1842–March 19, 1927)[95]

318. Plunk, M.F., child of S.C. & L.A. Plunk (August 21, 1873–August 16, 1876)

319. Plunk, Mary E., wife of E. Lawson Plunk (August 8, 1871–December 10, 1961)[96]

320. Plunk, Moriah (1834–1915) Although this is a marked grave, one source lists Moriah as "Mariah" and shows her dates as being from March 8, 1834 to December 31, 1915, and she being the daughter of George Plunk.[97]

321. Plunk, S.C. (January 5, 1845–February 14, 1905)[98]

322. Plunk, Samuel, infant of W.L. & Susie Plunk (no dates)

323. Plunk, Soferia J., wife of David F. Plunk (1883–1960)

324. Putman, Alie (January 20, 1845–December 21, 1919)[99]

325. Putman, Henry E., son of J.F. & M.E. Putman (October 13, 1870–December 29, 1870)

92. According to the death records of McNairy County, Tennessee, Lawson Plunk died from typhoid fever under the treatment of Dr. William Henry Hodges. This cause of death somewhat conflicts with the oral tradition that Plunk was injured in the 1909 tornado and eventually died of his wounds. However, the author admits that it is possible that Plunk became sick with typhoid fever during his recuperation. *McNairy County, Tennessee Death Book, 1908-1912.* McNairy County Records Commission.

93. According to the death records of McNairy County, his first name was Elijah.

94. Kizzie Dunn is identified as Catherine M. Dunn in the marriage records of McNairy County, Tennessee.

95. L.A. Plunk was Levinia "Vina" Mason, the daughter of James Mason and wife Margaret Priscilla Mason. She was married to Samuel C. Plunk on or about February 1, 1868, with Alfred Monroe Plunk acting as bondsman for this marriage.

96. Mary Elizabeth "Mollie" Gage married Elijah Lawson Plunk on November 5, 1899, with Justice of the Peace F.J. Floyd officiating and Alfred Monroe Plunk acting as bondsman.

97. Kennedy, *Unmarked Graves in McNairy County, Tennessee.*

98. Samuel C. Plunk was a private in Company B of the U.S. Sixth Tennessee Cavalry, having enlisted and mustered in on June 18, 1863.

99. Alie Putman was the daughter of Martin Putman and never married.

326. Putman, J.E. (July 10, 1874–September 15, 1874)
327. Putman, John F. (August 23, 1841–July 29, 1921)[100]
328. Putman, John O., son of J.F. & M.E. Putman (April 22, 1880–November 16, 1887)
329. Putman, Martha E., wife of John F. Putman (April 29, 1844–November 8, 1922)
330. Putman, Martin (August 20, 1818–February 2, 1900)[101]
331. Putman, Tulitha (March 25, 1843–March 8, 1900)[102]
332. Putman, W.A. (August 1849–February 1925)[103]
333. Rankin, Bettie E., wife of Francis M. Rankin (1834–1926)
334. Rankin, Francis M., *Q.M. Sgt, Co. B, Sixth Tennessee Cavalry, U.S.A.* (1836–1890)
335. Rankin, Frank M, son of F.M. & B.E. Rankin (September 15, 1871–May 20, 1894)[104]
336. Rankin, John Dodridge (1816–1870) *Unmarked*
337. Rankin, Mary Kerby (1820–1880s) *Unmarked*
338. Robinson, David Harl, brother of Oneva Robinson (February 13, 1917–December 22, 1988)
339. Robinson, Oneva, sister of David Harl Robinson (December 22, 1914–December 1991)
340. Robison, A. Tucker (August 5, 1906–October 22, 1967)
341. Robison, Charity Ann, wife of L.C. Robison (1868–1948)[105]
342. Robison, J. Frank (October 20, 1918–November 14, 1992) *PFC, U.S. Army, World War II*

100. John F. Putman was a private and later sergeant in Company B of the U.S. Sixth Tennessee Cavalry having enlisted on August 25, 1862, and having mustered in on November 13, 1863. Putman married Martha E. Lane, the daughter of Thomas Lane and Jane A. Lane. She was the sister of James Simpson "Simp" Lain. Interestingly, the names Lane and Lain were often used interchangeably. The Putmans were married on December 23, 1866, with the Reverend Wilson A. McHolstead officiating and Captain Elijah J. Hodges acting as bondsman.

101. Martin F. Putman's wife was already deceased by 1860.

102. Tulitha J. Putman was the daughter of Martin Putman and never married.

103. William A. Putman was the son of Martin Putman.

104. According to the late Haven Garner, Frank Rankin was accidently shot and died during an operation at home to retrieve the bullet.

105. Her death certificate lists her dates as (September 25, 1868–June 24, 1948), and her parents as Samuel and Lavina (Mason) Plunk. Charity Ann (Plunk) Robison Death Certificate No. 13266. Tennessee Death Records 1914–1955. <familysearch.org>

343. Robison, Gary Lynn (August 9, 1956–December 19, 1998) *U.S. Army*

344. Robison, J.F. (March 14, 1892–October 23, 1918)

345. Robison, L.C. (July 11, 1866–August 6, 1927)[106]

346. Robison, Martha, wife of Hayse Robison (January 11, 1922–April 20, 1999)

347. Robison, William Hayse (June 14, 1923–December 17, 1991) *PFC, U.S. Army, World War II*

348. Rouse, infant son of J.M. & M. (born & died May 17, 1874)

349. Rouse, J.M. (August 27, 1852–March 5, 1907)[107]

350. Rouse, Lydia H., daughter of J.M. & M. Rouse (September 27, 1875–December 16, 1875)

351. Rouse, Mary, wife of J.M. Rouse (June 22, 1850–April 1906)

352. Smith, Bethel S. (February 28, 1947–December 20, 1988)

353. Smith, Curt James (no dates)

354. Smith, Daisy Kathleen (no dates)

355. Smith, Frances, daughter of J.W. & May Smith (December 18, 1920–September 30, 1921)

356. Smith, Fred B. (January 1, 1915–May 14, 1996)

357. Smith, Infant daughter of Lee Roy & Lora E. (May 7, 1934–June 3, 1934)

358. Smith, Lee Roy (September 11, 1903–September 21, 1970)

359. Smith, Leonard Riley (no dates)

360. Smith, Lora E., wife of Lee Roy Smith (January 14, 1909–January 11, 1976)

361. Stansell, John William (May 15, 1871–June 16, 1926)[108]

362. Starks, Almeda, wife of Elijah Starks (1849–1937)

106. Larkin Calloway Robison was the son of Genile (?) and Margerete (Martin) Robison. He married Charity Ann Plunk on November 17, 1887, with William Barney Malone officiating and W.W. King acting as bondsman. Larkin Caloway Robison Death Certificate No. 20472. Id.

107. J.M. Rouse's wife is believed to have been Mary Mickens. There is a marriage record for the couple with a marriage date of November 21, 1872, with Justice of the Peace Jacob Lowrance officiating and A.M. Neal acting as bondsman. A transcription error shows the last name as "Rowsey."

108. According to one individual who identified herself as his daughter, Mr. John William Stansell was to be committed to Western State Mental Hospital on June 16, 1926, and when he was left alone in his room to gather his personal effects, he took his straight-razor and cut his own throat. The home remains today and is located just off Highway 45 leaving Finger.

363. Starks, Elijah (1845–1907)[109]
364. Starks, John (1880–1950)
365. Starks, Tennie, wife of John Starks (1898–1987)
366. Stewart, Mary A., daughter of of J.F. & A.M.J. Stewart (April 8, 1870–January 9, 1871)
367. Stewart, Nancy A., daughter of J.F. and A.M.J. Stewart (May 27, 1866–January 12, 1871)[110]
368. Stout, Enna Etheridge (1889–1972)
369. Stout, Evelyn, daughter of Elvis & Enna Stout (born & died July 16, 1924)
370. Stout, Hugh Elvis (1894–1973)
371. Stout, Louis A. (May 8, 1871–January 28, 1958)
372. Stout, Martha E., wife of Louis A. Stout (July 8, 1888–February 25, 1970
373. Stout, Rachel Orra Elizabeth, wife of L.A. Stout (October 18, 1870–January 3, 1911)
374. Strickland, Bertha N. (January 9, 1919–January 3, 1988)[111]
375. Strickland, Debbie K. (September 7, 1957–October 3, 2002)
376. Strickland, Leslie "Buddy" (April 28, 1944–March 19, 1993)
377. Surratt, Eugene (September 30, 1879–March 18, 1943)
378. Tedford, infant daughter of E.S. & Sarah Ada (born & died 1917)[112]
379. Tedford, A.K. (November 21, 1859–April 17, 1927)[113]

109. Elijah W. Starks married Loutisha Almeda Floyd, the daughter of Harmon Floyd and wife Lucrecia Floyd, on November 13, 1879, with the Reverend Wilson A. McHolstead officiating and W.T. Bell acting as bondsman. Mrs. Starks' first name has also been spelled as "Lutecia."

110. A.M.J. Stewart was Antione Jane McIntyre, the daughter of Robert Thompson McIntyre and Sarah Jane Weaver. She was born in 1841 and married J.F. Stewart. They moved to Texas after 1871 and she died in Boston, Texas.

111. Bertha Strickland was the mother of Buddy Strickland and Bethel Smith, both buried at Mount Carmel.

112. Her parents were Ernest and Sarah Ada (Morris) Tedford. McNairy County Archives, compiler. "McNairy County, Tennessee Marriage Records, ca. March 1861–October 1961." <mcnairytnhistory.com/images/Grooms_M-Z_Mar_1861_Oct_1961.pdf> They were married September 14, 1914. They were also listed as parents of an adult child, Jewell (Tedford) Young, who was buried at Sweetlips Cemetery. Jewell (Tedford) Young Death Certificate No. 20944. Tennessee Death Records 1914–1955. <familysearch.org>

113. Allen Kennie Tedford, the son of Alex W. Tedford and wife Mary Jane (Robbins) Tedford, married Jennie Bell Lain on November 24, 1885, with Justice of the Peace William Barney Malone officiating and J.V. Tedford acting as bondsman.

380. Tedford, Jennie Bell Lain, wife of A.K. Tedford (June 19, 1869–September 27, 1919)

381. Vanwart, Beulah, wife of Lewis A. Vanwart (May 15, 1921–April 18, 1994)[114]

382. Vanwart, Lewis A. (October 16, 1928–April 16, 1994) *ATC, U.S. Navy, Korea*

383. Walker, infant son of W.C. & S. (born & died December 15, 1876)

384. Walker, Curtis A. (July 24, 1872–February 23, 1959)

385. Walker, George R., son of W.C. & S. Walker (May 17, 1870–October 22, 1875)

386. Walker, Hubert B., son of C.A. & Melinda Walker (December 22, 1895–June 17, 1896)

387. Walker, James H., son of W.C. & S. Walker (November 26, 1874–March 21, 1895)[115]

388. Walker, Melinda, wife of C.A. Walker (November 13, 1868–November 21, 1898)

389. Walker, Mary Lou, wife of C.A. Walker (February 10, 1882–April 24, 1969)

390. Walker, Susan, wife of W.C. Walker (October 10, 1841–August 16, 1904)

391. Walker, William C. *Co. B, Sixth Tennessee Cavalry, U.S.A.*[116]

392. Walker, Winnie M., daughter of C.A. & Melinda Walker (February 3, 1898–January 7, 1899)

393. Wamble, infant son of J.M. & M.A. (born & died February 14, 1854)

394. Wamble, Mary, daughter of A.R. & Bettie Wamble (January 26, 1910–October 20, 1910)[117]

114. Beulah Vanwart was the daughter of Arthur Marion Douglas "Whig" McCann and Celia (Weaver) McCann.

115. His full name was James Harvey Walker.

116. William Carroll Walker (December 11, 1841–October 1, 1929). He and wife Susan Walker were the parents of Murry F. Walker and W.H. "Tobe" Walker. William Carroll Walker Death Certificate No. 25050. Id. William C. Walker card in Organization Index to Pension Files of Veterans Who Served Between 1861–1900 (Tennessee, Cavalry, Regiment Sixth, Company B) <fold3.com>

117. According to the death records of McNairy County, Mary Wamble died on October 26, 1910, of diphtheria, with Dr. William Henry Hodges attending. *McNairy County, Tennessee Death Book, 1908-1912.* McNairy County Records Commission.

395. Ward, John B. (August 8, 1847–October 10, 1915)[118]
396. Ward, Mary Ann Loumiza, wife of N.G. Ward (January 7, 1828–August 1, 1900)
397. Ward, Nathan G. (June 15, 1821–January 6, 1891)[119]
398. Ward, Thankful C., wife of John B. Ward (April 4, 1850–January 24, 1874)[120]
399. Weaver, J.F., son of R.M. & M.A. Weaver (January 12, 1872–October 5, 1875)[121]
400. Wells, Ernest (January 26, 1893–April 6, 1921) *Son of Fred Wells and Laura Love*
401. White, Tabitha Eunice Hodges (August 8, 1820–January 5, 1853) *Unmarked*
402. Whitt, Adell, daughter of W.H. & Z.R. Whitt (November 1, 1918–October 31, 1919)
403. Whitt, Andrew Carroll (1849–1925)
404. Whitt, Olar Ethmy, daughter of J.W. & Sarah Whitt (September 24, 1909–August 4, 1911)[122]
405. Whitt, William Harrison (February 8, 1889- June 18, 1926)[123]
406. Whitt, Zelphia Roberta, wife of William H. Whitt (1886–1965)
407. Whorton, Lizzie, wife of P.E. Whorton (1883–1971)

118. John B. Ward, the son of Nathan Gilbert Ward and Mary Ann Loumiza Ward, married Thankful C. Rankin on September 25, 1870, with Justice of the Peace Jacob Lowrance officiating and Thomas H. Ward acting as bondsman. Thankful was the daughter of J.D. and Mary Rankin.

119. Nathan G. Ward was a child of Matthew and Esther Ward and he spent his young years on Mount Carmel at the settlement established there by his parents and their neighbors.

120. Thankful C. Rankin married John B. Ward on September 25, 1870, with Justice of the Peace Jacob Lowrance officiating and Thomas H. Ward acting as bondsman.

121. R.M. and M.A. Weaver are Robert McMillan Weaver and wife Mary A. Highfield Womble Weaver. Mary A. Highfield was first married to Manley Womble, and they had sons William A. Womble, Thomas J. Womble and Isom Womble. Robert McMillam Weaver married Mary A. Highfield Womble in September 1867 and had sons J.F. Weaver and Lee Andrew Weaver.

122. According to the death records of McNairy County, her name was Paralee Whitt, a child who died of dysentery while attended to Dr. Nathaniel A. Tucker. *McNairy County, Tennessee Death Book, 1908-1912.* McNairy County Records Commission.

123. William Harrison Whitt, the son of Andrew Carroll Whitt, married Zilphia McIntyre Sanders on March 3, 1909, with Justice of the Peace J.E. Barham officiating and Charles B. Steadman acting as bondsman. Zilphia (Zelphia) was first married to Radie Sanders. Mr. Sanders died during the typhoid breakout in 1907.

408. Whorton, P.E. (1881–1960)[124]
409. Willis, Bert Orvil Leslie, son of Walter & Esta Willis (September 7, 1970–February 11, 1971)
410. Wilson, Myrtle Elizabeth (November 13, 1930–February 18, 2011)
411. Womble, Allen R. (July 4, 1885–July 30, 1909)[125]
412. Womble, Infant daughter of W.B. & M.E. (born & died April 16, 1897)
413. Womble, Jessie T., son of W.B. & M.E. Womble (February 14, 1896–May 14, 1896)
414. Womble, Lucy E., wife of T.J. Womble (October 10. 1860–March 25, 1926)[126]
415. Womble, Mary E. Beene, wife of W.B. Womble (April 6, 1866–July 2, 1904)[127]
416. Womble, Mary E. Case, wife of W.B. Womble (April 23, 1877–?)[128]
417. Womble, T.J. (December 11, 1858–September 3, 1939)
418. Womble, W.B. (July 20, 1856–July 28, 1940)
419. Young, Addie, wife of William S. Young (1878–1966)
420. Young, Catherine, wife of Johnson Young (circa 1840–August 1884)
421. Young, J.R.F. (July 17, 1872–March 20, 1909)
422. Young, Johnson (February 25, 1835–March 14, 1880)
423. Young, Lessie G. (November 5, 1917–February 7, 1953)[129]
424. Young, Lottie M. (July 1913–October 1914)
425. Young, Lude (1832–1908)
426. Young, Martha, wife of Stephen Young (October 10, 1803–May 18, 1886)
427. Young, William A. (August 1905–September 1905)

124. P.E. Whorton married Lizzie Brown on September 26, 1903, with Justice of the Peace N.R. Ward officiating and R.B. Whorton acting as bondsman. The Whortons had no children and lived on the corner of Talbott (Mill) Street and Apple Street in Finger.

125. Allen R. Womble married Bettie Naylor on July 23, 1905, with Justice of the Peace C.C. Plunk officiating and Horry Hodges acting as bondsman.

126. Louiza E. "Lucy" Walker married Thomas J. Womble on January 17, 1884, with Capt. Elijah J. Hodges officiating and N.G. Ward acting as bondsman.

127. Mary E. Beene married William Womble on December 31, 1879, with Justice of the Peace Robert Thompson McIntyre officiating.

128. Mary E. Case married William Womble on December 30, 1907, with J.E. "Ed" Barham officiating.

129. Lessie G. Young was the daughter of Charlie B. Griffin and wife Ludie W. Griffin and the former wife of Horry Young. Her son was Charles Young.

428. Young, William S. (1868–1952)[130]
429.–495. Unknown

To date, there may be found about 67 discernible unmarked graves located in the cemetery.[131] In 1991, that number was over 100. Since that time, about 34 graves have been recovered from anonymity and disregard. The articles from the *McNairy County Independent Appeal* previously quoted in Chapter One were the first written sources discovered that identified graves which were never marked or were no longer marked. After a review of surviving funeral home records from the 1930s and 1940s, family Bible records, and other private records, a number of other names were retrieved from the unknown column. Finally, members of families and those who were decorating unmarked and unidentified graves were consulted for the names of these graves, with better than fair results.

The following individuals are believed to be buried in Mount Carmel Cemetery according to family lore, tradition, records, and circumstantial evidence:

1. Elisha Hodges (November 24, 1794–September 1, 1847)
2. Millie (Ward) Hodges (July 3, 1790–May 19, 1859)
3. Powell Sipes (born circa 1826), the father of Jennie (Sipes) Holland
4. Sarah (Gage) Sipes (born circa 1833), the mother of Jennie (Sipes) Holland
5. Esther Ward
6. Matthew Ward
7. Samuel White, husband of Tabitha Eunice (Hodges) White
8. Ellen (Hubanks) McIntyre
9. Jesse Hodges (February 11, 1754–March 18, 1842)
10. Elizabeth (Collins) Hodges (August 28, 1760–January 6, 1842)
11. Sarah Elizabeth (Dodd) Hodges, first wife of Captain Horry Hodges (died August 7, 1858)
12. William Dodd, the father of Nancy Jane (Dodd) Hodges and Sarah Elizabeth (Dodd) Hodges (born circa 1808)

---

130. William Sherman Young was a farmer and blacksmith in Finger, Tennessee.

131. The author believes the unmarked graves to far exceed this number. Graves have been located in the woods around the cemetery.

13. Ailey Dodd, mother of Nancy Jane (Dodd) Hodges and Sarah Eliza-
    beth (Dodd) Hodges (she is also referred to Alcy Dodd) (born
    circa 1808)
14. William Cayson Hodges (born September 22, 1778)
15. Kiza Hodges (born circa 1780)

However, until further reliable and substantiating evidence can be
found to support these suppositions, they will have to remain just that,
suppositions.

Mt. Carmel Black Cemetery

It is unfortunate that we have little information regarding the black
section of the Mount Carmel Cemetery. We do not know when it began, if slaves or free blacks were its first occupants, or how many graves
eventually filled this section of the cemetery. However, some information is known about it. By the early 1930s, it was encircled by a white
painted wood slat fence. It was regularly visited by neighboring blacks
and the graves were well-maintained. When a funeral in the black community occurred at Mount Carmel, the meetinghouse was used by the
mourners to hold services.

According to older residents of the community in the 1980s, including John Robert McIntyre, Harriet (McCann) Rouse, Guy Brown, Luther Edward Talbott, and others, the black cemetery was rather large.
When thought out logically, this makes sense. Although there are few
blacks in north McNairy County today, there were many more at the
turn of the twentieth century. Given that fact, there is no known black
cemetery north of McNairy Station until one crosses the present-day
Chester County line. Therefore, it makes perfect sense that a significant
black cemetery would have existed at Mount Carmel. There were many
black families in the immediate vicinity, including but not limited to the
Vassar, Draper and Bass families. These families had members who lived
their entire lives near Mount Carmel Cemetery, and it would seem unusual for them to be buried elsewhere.

Sometime in the early to mid 1940s, a cemetery drive was constructed around the white portion of the cemetery, and the black cemetery was
tragically destroyed in the course of construction. The black section may

have become poorly kept but nonetheless, its destruction for the purpose of building a cemetery drive was unacceptable. In 2008, the cemetery drive was removed and the land was restored to cemetery space. The author is currently making efforts to determine the possible boundaries of the old black section of the cemetery. Certain portions of those boundaries were identified by the older residents mentioned above.

Currently, only one individual— Mrs. Lenora Derrick—can be identified with certainty as having been buried in this section. The author is making efforts to ascertain other black citizens whose earthly remains slumber in this section of old Mount Carmel Cemetery.

CHAPTER FIVE

A PHOTOGRAPHIC GALLERY
OF THOSE BURIED AT MOUNT CARMEL

Included in this work are a number of photographs of some of the hardy people and pioneers buried in Mount Carmel Cemetery. Some of these photographs exist where even biographical information is lacking. Careful examination of these images gives the reader much to ponder. Some of the faces are hard and appear knowing. They are the faces of tired, haggard individuals whose years have seen difficulty, hardship, toil, happiness, extreme sorrow in a world that could be harsh and unfriendly. Some of the faces are of the dead young. Theirs are soft and untested. Their lamp of life was extinguished long before it had the opportunity to burn brightly. These young people would go to their graves early and would remain forever young. The tombstone of twenty-three year old John R. Jones, buried at Mount Carmel, most probably sums up the feeling of many parents of recently deceased young people as it states: "How many hopes lie buried here?"

The inclusion of these photographs is to allow the reader to put faces with the names on old familiar tombstones. Having a face with which to identify the deceased gives the reader an identity and a starting point from which to begin to get to "know" the deceased. The dead are not given justice when the living can know only their names and dates from a cold slab of limestone, marble or granite. When life can be infused into that which is otherwise cold and indifferent, it allows the reader and the student of history and genealogy to better understand the deceased. Therefore, in an effort to bring some measure of life back to the otherwise lifeless names and statistics, the author commends the following photographs of some of those who slumber in the old Mount Carmel Cemetery.

Malissa America Coleman
wife of William Moses Beene

Mary Jane Beene
wife of Allen Louis Beene

Elmer and Nancy Virginia
(McCann) Cogdell

Ben Floyd

Charlie B. Griffin

Arl and Jessie (McCann) Davis

Michael Davis, son of
Arl and Jessie Davis

Captain Elijah J. Hodges and wife Nancy Jane (Dodd) Hodges

Horry Hodges   *Dr. William Henry Hodges*

Julia Ann Hodges

Maggie Hodges

Harvey Hodges

Ava Lee (McCann) Kaufman

Charlie Hugh Kirkpatrick

John T. Kirkpatrick and family

Mollie Kirkpatrick

Truman McCann

Arthur C. "Arter" McCann

William Andrew "Ander" McCann, wife
Elsie (Barnes) McCann

Ola McCann

Cordelia H. "Celia" (Weaver) McCann

A.D. McCann, Arthur Marion "Pat" McCann, and Jim Dell McCann

Family of John Absalom and Mary Roberta (Coleman) McIntyre. (Left to right) Top row: Zenar McIntyre, Adrian McIntyre. Bottom row: Sarah McIntyre, Mary (holding John Robert McIntyre), John, and Zelphia McIntyre

*Family of John Robert and Ollie Pearl
(McCann) McIntyre. Left to right: Mary
Helen McIntyre, Ollie, Lessie Eveline
McIntyre, Roy Robert McIntyre, and John.*

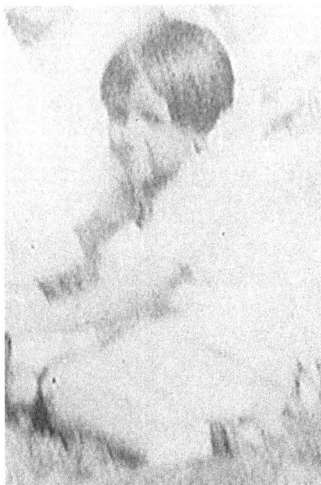

Audrey Roberta McIntyre

Vergie I. McIntyre

*Margaret (Beene) McIntyre
wife of James R. McIntyre*

Hubert U. McIntyre, his son Earl
McIntyre, and his wife Maggie L.
McIntyre

Charles Banner Peebles

J.N. "Neute" and Mary Jane Owen

Curtis A. and Mary Lou Walker

James Harvey Walker
son of W.C. and S. Walker

Zelphia Roberta (McIntyre) Whitt

Allen R. Womble

Thomas J. and Lucy E. Womble

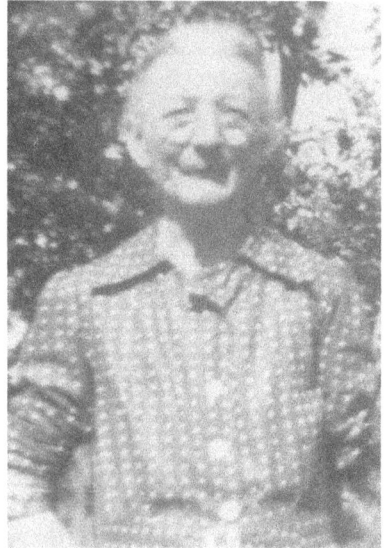

William Sherman Young   *Addie Young, wife of W.S. Young*

SOURCES CONSULTED

Allison, Judge John. *Notable Men of Tennessee: Personal and Genealogical with Portraits.* Atlanta, GA: Southern Historical Association, 1905.

American Wesleyan, November 8, 1881. The Archives and Historical Library of the International Center, The Wesleyan Church, Indianapolis, Indiana.

Angle, Paul M. *Bloody Williamson: A Chapter in American Lawlessness.* Chicago: University of Illinois Press, 1992.

Bigger, Elizabeth "Bessie" Abernathy (1875–1941), Scrapbooks, privately published in Jackson, Tennessee (microfilmed).

Claim for Widow's Pension (War of 1861) of Isabel J. Coleman, dated March 6, 1866. National Archives, Washington, D.C.

Cox, R. Harold, compiler. *Marriages of McNairy County, Tennessee, 1861–1911.* Selmer, TN: G & P Printing Services, 1989.

Gooch Funeral Home Records. Jack McConnico Memorial Library, Selmer, Tennessee.

Hand, Marvin. "Notes Taken While Talking to John Robert McIntyre at Finger, Tennessee," March 2, 1982.

Hodges Family Archives. Ben Davidson, Bingham, Illinois.

Kennedy, Nancy Wardlow, compiler. *Unmarked Graves in McNairy County, Tennessee.* Selmer, TN: Self-published, 2006.

Maness, Affidavit of Nancy, A Midwife, March 18, 1871. National Archives, Washington, D.C.

McCann, Kevin D. *Hurst's Wurst: Colonel Fielding Hurst and the Sixth Tennessee United States Cavalry.* Ashland City, TN: Cardinal Press, 1997.

McCann, Kevin D. *The McCanns of McNairy County, Tennessee: A History of the Descendants of John McCann Senior.* Ashland City, TN: Privately published, 1993.

McNairy County, Tennessee Death Book, 1908–1912. McNairy County Records Commission.

McNairy County Independent Appeal, April 25, 1913.

McNairy County Independent Appeal, September 12, 1913.

McNairy County Independent Appeal, March 25, 1921.

McNairy County Independent Appeal, September 8, 1922.

McNairy County Independent Appeal, September 12, 1924.

McNairy County Independent Appeal, February 12, 1926.

McNairy County Independent Appeal, May 20, 1927.

McNairy County Independent Appeal, August 4, 1939.

McNairy County Independent Appeal, August 13, 1939.

McNairy County Independent Appeal, September 27, 1940.

McNairy County Independent Appeal, November 21, 1941.

McNairy County, Tennessee Register of Deeds Office. Deed Book A, page 2.

McNairy County, Tennessee Register of Deeds Office. Deed Book K, page 758.

McNairy County, Tennessee Register of Deeds Office. Deed Book 27, page 522.

McNairy County, Tennessee Register of Deeds Office. Deed Book 42, page 86.

Moore, John Trotwood. *Tennesseans in the Civil War: A Military History of Confederate and Union Units with Available Rosters of Personnel, Part 1.* Nashville, TN: Civil War Centennial Commission, 1964.

Murry, *Affidavit of Elizabeth, A Midwife.* March 13, 1871. National Archives, Washington, D.C.

Neimann, Ruth Helen. *The Glory of a Common Man: A Biography.* Privately published, 1976.

Parsons, John Carlyle. *History of One Parsons Family.* 1938.

Pitts, Dr. Shawn. "McNairy County Brooms: Better and Cheaper Than Any Brought On," *Tennessee Folklore Society Bulletin*, Volume LXV, Number 2, Fall 2012, Knoxville, Tennessee.

Reed, Betty Sitton. *My Three Sons, Volume III: Beene-McIntyre and Allied Lines.* Memphis, TN: Privately published, 1985.

Talbott, John E., J.D. *Let's Call It Finger: A History of North McNairy County and Finger, Tennessee and Its Surrounding Communities.* Henderson, TN: Privately published, 2003.

Taylor, J.C. *Historical Articles.* Selmer, TN: Privately published, 1992.

The Selmer Post, April 24, 1903.

The Weekly Post, November 13, 1903.

Vaughan, A.J. *Personal Record of the Thirteenth Regiment, Tennessee Infantry, C.S.A.* Memphis, TN: S.C. Toof & Co. Press, 1897. Reprinted by Frank & Gennie Myers and Burke's Book Store, Memphis, Tennessee.

Whitehead, Marie F. *The History of the Lowrance Family.* Jack McConnico Memorial Library, Selmer, Tennessee.

Widow's Declaration to the Department at Washington for Army Pension of Isabel J. Coleman dated June 17, 1865. National Archives, Washington, D.C.

Conversations, Interviews, and Oral Histories

Guy Brown
Ben Davidson
Albert Floyd
Haven Garner
Marvin Hand
John Lloyd Harris

Hayes Hayre
Richard Leath
John Robert McIntyre
Lessie E. McIntyre
Roy R. McIntyre
Vivian A. McIntyre
Harriet McCann Rouse
Faye McIntyre Talbott
Luther E. Talbott
Clifford Young

ABOUT THE AUTHOR

JOHN E. TALBOTT was raised on Mount Carmel Hill just within view the Mount Carmel Cemetery. He lived on this old hill for twenty-five years, hunting its woods, roaming the hills, and helping to farm its red clay soils. He visited the old burying grounds on many occasions and gathered there with family to bury loved ones, to decorate graves, to clean and mow the grounds, and to learn. Mount Carmel Hill always held a special place in his heart and for his family. He grew from a young child to a grown man on this old hill. Many happy memories were made there.

Mr. Talbott attended McNairy and Chester County Schools and graduated from Freed-Hardeman University in 1995 with a Bachelor of Arts Degree in History and from the University of Memphis, Cecil C. Humphreys School of Law, with a Juris Doctor degree in 2002. He has taught history and geography in Chester and McNairy County schools and at Freed-Hardeman University as an adjunct professor. He has practiced law since 2003. He is the owner and managing partner of John E. Talbott & Associates, PLLC, in Henderson, Tennessee.

He is married to the former Michelle Leigh Smith, a native of Memphis, Tennessee, and a graduate of Lambuth University. They have two daughters, Ava Jewel Talbott and Claire Elisabeth Talbott. They reside in Finger, Tennessee. Mr. Talbott spends his spare time reading and researching Tennessee and Southern history and folklore.

www.ingramcontent.com/pod-product-compliance
Lightning Source LLC
Chambersburg PA
CBHW060355090426
42734CB00011B/2143

9780967125190